DEVELOPING STRATEGIES

STRATEGIES 3

AN INTEGRATED LANGUAGE COURSE FOR INTERMEDIATE STUDENTS

Brian Abbs
Ingrid Freebairn

Longman

Longman Group Limited
Longman House,
Burnt Mill, Harlow,
Essex CM20 2JE,
England

First published 1980
Fourth impression 1982
ISBN 0 582 51627 7

Acknowledgements

The publishers would like to thank the following for permission to reproduce copyright material:

Advisory Centre for Education (ACE) Ltd for an adapted extract from 'What do you expect from school?' in *Where*; Associated Newspapers Group Ltd for an adapted extract from 'Phone Call from Dino' in *Daily Mail* August 22nd, 1979; Bike Magazine for the adapted article 'What makes Eddie Kidd Jump?' by Mike Nicks in *Bike* No. 59, February 1978, reproduced by permission of Bike Magazine; the author's agents, Hughes Massie Ltd and Harold Ober Associates Inc for an extract from *Death on the Nile* by Agatha Christie copyright 1937, 1965 by Agatha Christie Mallowan; Collins Publishers for an adapted extract from the introduction to *Sleeping Murder* by Agatha Christie, Fontana Paperback; Guardian Newspapers Ltd for an adapted extract from 'Slow Train to China' by Angela Singer in *The Guardian* February 28th, 1979; Jetsave Ltd for adapted extracts from Jetsave Brochure 'Offer: Rocky Rendez-vous (a special eight day tour of the Rocky Mountains)'; Jobs Weekly for the adapted article 'Heroes' by Simon Walsh in *Jobs Weekly* Vol 1, No 25 copyright Jobs Weekly 1979; McGraw-Hill Book Company for an adapted extract from *The Brendan Voyage* by Tim Severin. Used with the permission of McGraw-Hill Book Company; Millington Books Ltd for adapted extracts from *Marilyn: a very personal story* by Norman Rosten; the author's agent for an adapted extract from page 75 of *Working For Free* by Sheila Moore, published by Severn House Publishers Ltd and Pan Books Ltd; Octopus Books Ltd for an adapted extract from *The Junior Encyclopedia of General Knowledge;* Penguin Books Ltd for an extract from the introduction to *Animal Farm* by George Orwell; Syndication International Ltd for adapted extracts from the article 'They Shouldn't Have Risked It' in *Daily Mirror* August 16th, 1979.

We are grateful to the following for permission to reproduce copyright photographs:

Alan Hutchinson Library for page 11 (left); All-Sport Photographic Ltd. for page 71; Anglo-Chinese Educational Institute for page 50 (right); Australian Information Service, London for pages 18/19; Avon Rubber Company Ltd., for page 107; Barnaby's Picture Library for pages 8 (2, 5 & 7), 10 (right), 23 (bottom right), 32, 36 (top), 64, 104 (1,2,4 & 6), 114 (left & middle left); BBC Copyright for pages 116 & 119 (top & middle); Biofotos for page 110 (left); Ann Bolt for page 123 (left); British Airways for page 121 (top); Camera Press Ltd., for pages 20, 23 (bottom middle), 36 (bottom), 50 (top left), 74 (left) & 122 (middle); J. Allan Cash Ltd., for pages 8 (8 & 9), 10 (left), 23 (bottom left), 36 (middle), 50 (bottom left), 59 (bottom), 76 & 108; Chris Davies for page 10 (middle right); Elizabeth Photo Library for pages 8 (3) & 104 (3 & 5); EMI Films Ltd., for pages 74/75; Humphrey Evans for page 91 (inset); GEC Telecommunications Ltd., for page 23 (middle left); Henry Grant Photos for pages 8 (1 & 6), 10 (middle left), 25 (5), 28, 41 & 84; Anwar Hussein for page 122 (left); Japan Information Centre for page 122 (right); Jetsave Ltd., for page 79; John Topham Picture Library for page 60; The Kobal Collection Ltd., for page 34; Lisa Mackson for page 25 (1,2,4 & 6); London Weekend Television for page 119 (bottom right); Pace Photographs for pages 25 (3); Photographers International for page 67 (left); Pictorial Press Ltd., for page 35; Picturepoint Ltd., for page 8 (4), 17 & 55; Popperfoto for pages 98 & 99; Post Office for page 23 (top); Pritchard Services Group for page 121 (bottom); Alan F. Raymond for page 66; Rex Features Ltd., for pages 33 & 67 (right); Robert Harding Associates for pages 90/91; Jane Freebairn-Smith for pages 119 (bottom left) & 123 (middle); Spectrum Colour Library for page 59 (top); Susan Griggs Agency Ltd., for pages 122/123; Swedish Embassy for page 123 (right); University College, London for page 40; Zefa Picture Library (UK) Ltd., for pages 11 (right), 23 (middle right) & 114 (middle right & right).

All photographs not listed above were taken by Chris Moyse.

We also wish to thank Am Admel for permission to use their name in the advertisement on page 22, and Unigate Dairies for permission to take location photography, on pages 26/27.

Designed by Stephen Pitcher

Illustrated by:- Tony Baskeyfield for page 107 (top left); Jon Davis for page 82/83; Richard Dunn for pages 42/43 & 50/51; Howard Levitt for page 106; Colin Mier for page 95; Paul Morton for pages 31, 47 & 63; Parkway Group for pages 10/11, 6,7,34,51 (top), 87,90,91,99 & 111; Stephen Pitcher for page 59.

Phototypeset in Times New Roman by Parkway Group, London and Abingdon

Printed in Hong Kong by Sheck Wah Tong Printing Press Ltd

We would like to express our gratitude to everyone who has helped to produce this book. In particular we would like to thank Eleanor Melville for her invaluable criticisms and suggestions on the different drafts. Also, we would like to thank all the members of the EFL division at Ealing College of Higher Education for their help and support in the development and testing of all the Strategies materials.

The Bates Family

Stanley (aged 50)

They live in Wandsworth, South London. He is a long-distance lorry-driver for an international transport firm. She is a receptionist in a doctor's surgery.

Marjorie (aged 47)

Richard (aged 27)

Richard is a sales representative for an office equipment firm. He is a widower. He lives in a small house in Wimbledon, together with his five-year-old son, Kevin.

Sandra (Sandy) (aged 22)

Sandy is a research assistant for London Television (LTV). She shares a flat with another girl in Wembley. She has a boyfriend, Mark, who also works at LTV.

David (Dave) (aged 16)

Dave goes to a comprehensive school in Wandsworth. He lives at home with his parents. His girlfriend, Carol, is 17 and is a hairdresser's assistant.

Contents

Unit 1 Richard starts again

Richard is the eldest of the Bates' children. He is 27 and works as a sales representative for an office equipment firm in London. His wife, Sheila, died last year in a car accident. Their five-year-old son, Kevin, is just about to start school.

When his wife died, Richard went to live with his parents who have a house in Wandsworth. His mother gave up her job to look after Kevin and Richard was able to carry on working.

Now, a year later, Richard wants to find a house of his own so that his mother can go back to her job, and so that he and Kevin can start to build a new life.

One day he sees an advertisement for a small house in Wimbledon, an attractive suburb in South London, not too far from his parents. The price is reasonable and there is a good school nearby where he can send Kevin.

He tells his parents about it one evening after work.

Wimbledon. Attractive older style terrace house close to shops and transport. Entrance hall, large living room, modern kitchen/breakfast room, two good size bedrooms, bathroom, full gas central heating, south facing rear garden.

Check

What do you know about Richard? (his age, wife, son, parents, job).
Where has he been living for the past year?
Why did his mother give up her job?
Why does Richard now want to find a house of his own?
Why does he want to look for a house in Wimbledon?
Why does the house sound suitable?

Listen and answer

What reasons does Richard give his mother for wanting to leave?
What does he say he is going to do about his job?

Discuss

Why is it tiring for older people to have a young child in the house?
What sort of practical problems do you think Richard will have when he moves into a house of his own with Kevin?

Description: people and places

Richard is a young man of 27 *who* works as a sales representative.

Richard is a young man of 27 *whose* wife died recently.

The Bates Family

Richard, a young man of 27:
– works as a sales representative
– lives alone with his son, Kevin
– his wife died recently

Sandy, a young girl of 22:
– has a job in a TV company
– shares a flat in Wembley
– her one ambition is to become a TV producer

Mr and Mrs Bates, a middle-aged couple:
– live in a house in Wandsworth
– both go out to work
– their family have nearly all grown up and left home

Dave, a teenager of 16:
– still goes to school
– lives at home with his parents
– his main interest is cycling

1. Write three sentences about each member of the Bates' family. Link the first statement about their age, with each of the other three facts, like this:
Richard is a … who … whose …

I have a brother *who* lives in Hong Kong.

I have an aunt *who* collects stamps.

I have a friend *whose* cat only drinks cold tea.

2. Think of something interesting to describe some or all of the following people. Copy the chart and write in the information next to each person. Then tell your partner about your family and friends.

There is a good school nearby *where* he can send Kevin.

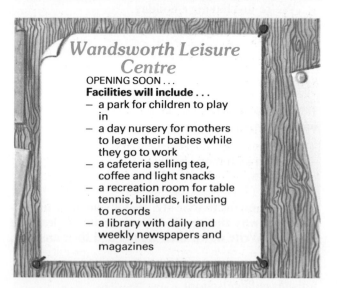

Wandsworth Leisure Centre
OPENING SOON . . .
Facilities will include . . .
– a park for children to play in
– a day nursery for mothers to leave their babies while they go to work
– a cafeteria selling tea, coffee and light snacks
– a recreation room for table tennis, billiards, listening to records
– a library with daily and weekly newspapers and magazines

3. Describe the facilities using where, **like this:**
There will be a park where children can play.

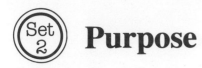

Purpose

> She gave up her job to look after Kevin.

Why come to Britain?

Photo Probe by Ann Clark

Our reporter, Ann Clark, interviewed some foreign people staying in London. She asked them the purpose of their visit.

1. 'To learn a bit more English.'
2. 'We're buying some antiques to take back to the States.'
3. 'I want to get experience of working abroad.'
4. 'We're just having a holiday.'
5. 'My main purpose is to make some business contacts.'
6. 'We've got tickets for the Wimbledon tennis finals.'
7. 'Actually, I'm studying law at London University.'
8. 'My girlfriend lives in London.'

1. Explain why all the people are in Britain. Work with a partner, like this:

– Why has she gone/come to Britain?
– To learn a bit more English.

2. In groups of five or six, make your own investigation of why the people in your group are learning English. Write down their names and their answers, like this:

Sumiko – to work in the computer industry when she finishes college/school.
Carlos – to get a job in a tourist office when he returns to Madrid.

3. Collect the names of the people in your class who have the same reasons for learning English. Find out the two most popular reasons for learning English.

He wants to find a house of his own so that his mother can go back to her job.

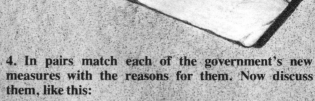

Mr David Bates
104 Maple Street
Islington
London N1

Your checklist of the new government measures in the pipeline.

This is what they plan to do and they plan to do it quickly:

* LOWER MORTGAGE RATES
* CUT INCOME TAX AT ALL LEVELS
* RAISE THE SCHOOL LEAVING AGE
* INVEST MORE MONEY IN DAY NURSERIES
* IMPROVE INDUSTRIAL RELATIONS
* INTRODUCE A DOCTOR'S CONSULTATION FEE

And this is WHY they say they are going to do it:

'There won't be so many unemployed school leavers.'
'More women can go out to work.'
'People can buy their own homes.'
'There will be more incentive for people to work.'
'People won't abuse the National Health Service so much.'
'There will be fewer strikes.'

4. In pairs match each of the government's new measures with the reasons for them. Now discuss them, like this:

– Why are the government going to ... ?
– So that there will be ...
          people won't ...
          can't ...

5. Write down two measures that your government has introduced recently and write two sentences like this:

The government has recently introduced a measure to . . ./so that . . . .

Give a reason for each measure.

People like you

Montgomery Brooks
from New York, U.S.A.

'I'm a professional
dancer – modern dance,
that is. I've always
wanted to work with the
Contemporary Dance
Theatre in London. Now
I've got the chance and
I'm thrilled I've never
been to Britain before.'

Name: Kathy Ng
Nationality: Thai
Age: 22
Occupation: Ground
hostess
with
Singapore
Airlines

Luisa Albini is a housewife
who comes from Udine in
the north-west of Italy, not
far from Venice. 'I studied
English at school but I've
forgotten quite a lot. I'd like
to keep it up so that I can
help my children with their
homework, and also so that
I can manage when we travel
abroad. I watch English and
American films on tele-
vision to keep in touch with
the language, but perhaps I
ought to take classes to
learn to speak it fluently.'

Name: Hanzi
Zimmerman
Age: 15
Hair: Red
Eyes: Blue
Hometown: Mannheim,
Germany
Ambition: To travel
and use his
languages

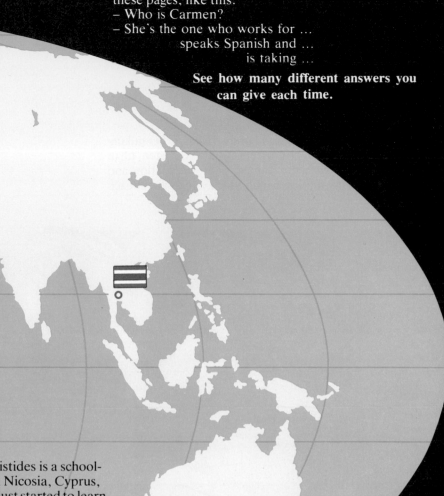

these pages, like this:
- Who is Carmen?
- She's the one who works for ...
                speaks Spanish and ...
                        is taking ...

**See how many different answers you
can give each time.**

Carmen Castro is a
chemist who works for a
large chemical company
in Recife, Brazil.
Carmen speaks Spanish
and Portuguese fluently.
'I'm now taking evening
classes to improve my
English. It's more
important now to speak
English in my job.'

Takis Aristides is a schoolboy from Nicosia, Cyprus,
who has just started to learn
English at school. His main
aim is to be able to read
English pop-music maga-
zines. He doesn't like his
English classes very much.
His father, a banker, would
like him to study harder so
that he can go to a British
University.

2. Ask and answer these questions:
    Why does Carmen want to take evening
classes in English? (To ...)

Why does Kathy need to be able to speak English?
Why does Montgomery want to go to Britain?
What is Hanzi's main ambition?
Why does Takis' father want him to work harder at
    his English?
Why does Luisa want to keep up her English?

11

Roleplay

In pairs. Choose two of the people on the map. Imagine that they meet for the first time at an informal party. Act out the conversation between them. Introduce yourselves, say where you come from, what you do and so on. Use the information you have read about each person.

Writing

Now write a short paragraph describing Shirley's family. Start like this:

Shirley comes from a large family of ...

 Listening

Shirley comes from a large family. Listen to her talking about her brothers and sisters. While you listen, fill in a family tree with the names, ages, occupation and any other information which Shirley gives about each of them.

Oral exercises

1. Finding the owner

Look at the pictures.

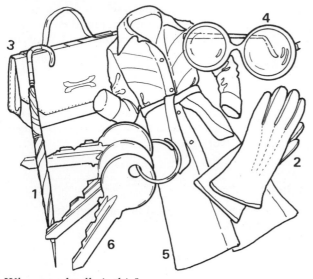

Whose umbrella is this?
Oh, it's mine. Sorry.

Whose gloves are these?
Oh, they're mine. Sorry.

2. Admiring possessions

Look at the pictures.

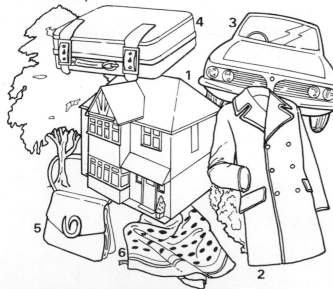

Mm. I wonder whose house that is?
I don't know. It's lovely, isn't it.

Mm. I wonder whose coat that is.
I don't know. It's smart, isn't it.

3. Looking at job applications

Mm, let's see … this girl speaks French.
Yes, someone who speaks French fluently could be useful.

What about this one – he says he can speak Spanish.
Yes, someone who speaks Spanish fluently could be useful.

And this one has Russian as a second language.
Ah, this one's got Italian.
This girl has a degree in German.
This man actually speaks Chinese.

4. Meeting new people

Come and meet Carmen. She speaks Spanish and Portuguese.
Oh, someone who speaks Spanish and Portuguese. That's interesting.

And that's Montgomery over there. He dances professionally, you know.
Oh, someone who dances professionally. That's interesting.

And that's Kathy. She comes from Thailand.
And you must meet Dave. He's keen on speed cycling.
And that's his sister, Sandy. She has a job in television.
And that man in the corner works on an oil rig.

5. Questioning reasons

I've come to St Anton for the skiing.
So you've come just to ski, have you?

I like meeting new people.
So you've come just to meet new people, have you?

I want to get some exercise.
I like watching the ice-skating.
I like tobogganing.
I enjoy the night life here.
I enjoy the fresh air.

Unit 2 Richard settles down

Richard has now bought the small house in Wimbledon and has moved in with Kevin. His mother, Mrs Bates, telephones to find out how they are both settling down.

MRS BATES: ... how are you settling down?

RICHARD: Oh, we're still in a bit of a mess but Kevin seems to like it here.

MRS BATES: That's good. Is there a garden for him to play in?

RICHARD: Yes, we've got a small garden which is a bit untidy at the moment. It's not big enough for him to play football in but it's all right. And of course there's Wimbledon Common which is quite near.

MRS BATES: Have you found a school for Kevin?

RICHARD: Yes, there's one just round the corner. They say it's one of the best schools in the area.

MRS BATES: That's good. So you like it there, do you, Richard?

RICHARD: Yes, it's got everything we need – shops, cinemas, restaurants. There's even a theatre, you know, which people say is very good.

Check

What opportunities or facilities are there for:
– Kevin to play
– Kevin to go to school
– entertainment and leisure?

 Listen and answer

How does Mrs Bates show that she is interested and concerned about Richard and Kevin?
Why will Wimbledon be crowded in July?
Does Wimbledon sound an interesting place to live?

Discuss

What sort of town do you live in? Is it large or small?
Do you think it is an attractive place to live?
What sort of place is nice for children to grow up in?

Set 1

Description: facts

high	higher	highest
big	bigger	biggest
large	larger	largest

Fabulous facts about the world's ...

...highest mountains

Peak	Height above sea level (in metres/feet)
Everest	8,848 (29,029)
Godwin Austen	8,611 (28,251)
Kanchenjunga	8,586 (28,169)

...biggest continents

Continent	Area (in square kilometres/ miles)
Asia	44,426,000 (17,153,000)
Africa	30,233,000 (11,673,000)
North America	24,955,000 (9,635,000)

...largest islands

Island	Area (in square kilometres/ miles)
Greenland	2,175,592 (840,000)
New Guinea	821,324 (317,115)
Borneo	746,543 (288,242)

...largest lakes

Lake	Continent	Area in square kilometres/miles
Caspian Sea	Europe/Asia	423,400 (163,500)
Lake Superior	North America	82,300 (31,800)
Lake Victoria	Africa	74,664 (28,282)

...longest rivers

River	Continent	Length in kilometres/miles
Nile	Africa	6,700 (4,160)
Amazon	South America	6,300 (3,900)
Yangtse	Asia	5,000 (3,100)
Zaire	Africa	4,400 (2.700)
Missouri	North America	4,370 (2,700)

...weather

The hottest place on earth is Azizia, a town in a hilly farming area of Libya. The world's record temperature was recorded there in 1922 – 57.7°C (135.83°F). But several other places have a higher average temperature, including Death Valley in California, and parts of Western Australia. The coldest place is Antarctica, where a temperature of – 88.3°C (– 126.94°F) has been recorded. The wettest place is on Kauai Island, Hawaii, which has more than 330 rainy days a year. Reunion Island in the Indian Ocean had the heaviest downpour ever recorded – 1.870 mm (73.62 in.) in 24 hours. The driest place is part of the Atacama Desert in Chile where little rain falls.

1. In pairs, describe the following, like this:

The Nile is the longest river in the world.
New Guinea is the second largest island in the world.

The Nile	The Amazon	The Caspian Sea
Asia	Antarctica	The Missouri
New Guinea	The Yangtse	The Atacama Desert
Africa	Greenland	Kauai Island

2. Write about your country. Give facts to describe:

a lake	a street	a mountain
a city	an island	a university
a river	a cathedral	

Description: opinions

interesting	more interesting	most interesting
beautiful	more beautiful	most beautiful
impressive	more impressive	most impressive
attractive	more attractive	most attractive
good	better	best
bad	worse	worst

THOSE FABULOUS PLACES WITH STRANGE-SOUNDING NAMES . . . continuing our occasional series of travel impressions.
by Monica Musgrave

I Fell in Love with Crete

The island of Crete is perhaps most famous for its history. The Palace of Knossos is certainly one of the most impressive sights in the world. But Crete has more to offer tourists than just history. The wild countryside, the rugged mountains, the coloured fishing boats, the beautiful sunsets are still printed on my memory.

And at the heart of it all is Aghios Niklaos, a most picturesque village situated on the north coast of the island. The attractive waterside bars and the busy tavernas vibrate with bouzouki music until the small hours. Speak to the friendly local people and they will show you where to eat the most delicious local food. Of course, like other Greek islands, Crete is very crowded in the high season. But the swimming is very good and the beaches are as clean as any you will find.

Nobody has ever gone to Crete without wanting to go back again, again and again.

1. You are talking to Monica Musgrave. Ask what she thought of:

the Palace of Knossos
the local people there
the beaches
the food

Aghios Niklaos
the swimming
her holiday in general

Ask and answer like this:

What did you think of ...?
Did you like ...?
Was/were the ... good?

Yes, | it was / they were | one of the most ... / some of the most ...

I have ever | seen / been to / met | in the world.

2. In pairs ask and answer about:

- the most interesting book you've read for some time
- the most frightening film you remember
- the funniest play or film you've seen recently
- the most exciting piece of music you've listened to for some time
- the closest you've ever been to an accident
- the stupidest thing you've ever done
- the best disco you've ever been to
- the most beautiful view you've ever seen
- the most beautiful place you've ever been to
- the most delicious meal you can remember

Descriptions: opinions and facts

Corinne Leslie's Food Talk

Britain's liveliest food columnist finds out the truth.

Is it really true what they say about the food in Britain?

* The vegetables are always too soggy.
* There are not enough restaurants where you can eat well, cheaply *and* take the children.
* They put too many things on the plate at the same time.
* There is too much salt in everything.
* There are too few places where you can eat after midnight.

Well, those are some of the things they say, but now take a look at this guide to restaurants in a suburb of London and see for yourself if the criticisms are justified.

LA TRATTORIA
Cheerful and friendly south Italian style restaurant. Mama Peroni serves while Papa makes delicious home-made pasta in the kitchen. Children welcome but you must book. Take your own wine. Open Sundays.

LEGS DIAMOND
Take a trip down Memory Lane to the gangster days in the city of Chicago. It's trendy (with a disco at weekends) but you can take the kids. Best hamburgers in town served by a brisk and friendly young staff dressed up as gangsters and their girlfriends. Go and enjoy the fun. Closed Mondays.

LES TROIS FRÈRES
Eating is a serious business in this very smart and very expensive French restaurant. A lunchtime favourite for businessmen with expense accounts but, even for the average pocket, it's worth living on bread and cheese for a week just to taste the delicious food.

LITTLE AGORA
A little bit of the Athens plaka in the midst of a suburb of London. Try the stuffed vine leaves, sip the retsina, close your eyes and you could be in Greece. Open after midnight so it's ideal if you want to eat after a show. Closed Sundays and Mondays. Unlicenced so take your own retsina.

1. Look at the guide and find a restaurant:

which serves ... American food
French food
expensive food
home-made pasta

which seems ... lively
friendly
sophisticated
suitable for teenagers

where you can take ... children
businessmen
people who like a relaxed atmosphere

where you can go ... after midnight
on Sundays
to dance

In pairs ask and answer, like this:

Is there a restaurant which/where ...
There's a restaurant called ... which/where ...

2. In groups collect any criticisms you may have of the following:

living in a big city like London
living in the country
a popular holiday resort
television in your country
your education.

Make your criticisms like this:

... is far too ... for me
It's not ... enough
There's not enough ...

3. You are planning an end of term meal out for your class or group in your area. Discuss where you could go.

Development

Welcome to Sydney

Sydney is Australia's oldest, largest and liveliest state capital with a population of over 3,000,000. It is a colourful, modern city but it has also a natural beauty with green parkland and perhaps the world's most beautiful deep-water harbour.

As well as being famous for its modern buildings and roads, there are many places of historical interest in Sydney. For example, Mrs Macquarie's Chair, the area called the Rocks dating back to the early nineteenth century, and the attractive terrace houses of Paddington, are all close to the harbour and the city centre.

Sydney has many attractions which tourists can enjoy – surf beaches, a zoo, Koala Bear Park and an Opera House which is situated at the water's edge. Some say that this is one of the most beautiful examples of modern architecture in the world. For further entertainment there is a wide variety of restaurants, theatres, nightclubs, sports and social clubs. There is also a very efficient network of communications within the city, including an underground railway, buses and taxis. Sydney has a very pleasant, temperate climate. The average temperature in summer is 21.7°C, and in winter 12.6°C.

There are few places in the world where a visitor can find such a rich variety of natural and historical beauty, entertainment and culture. Ask any Sydneysider about his city and he'll say there's no place like it!

Check

Use the headings below
to make notes about
Sydney.

Population:
Natural beauty:
Historical sights:
Tourist attractions:
Entertainment:
Transport system:
Climate:

Discuss

HOW WELL DO YOU KNOW YOUR CITY?

In pairs, ask and answer questions about your city. Make notes of the answers in your notebooks under the different headings.

NAME OF CITY

GEOGRAPHICAL LOCATION	Is it situated in the north/south/east/west or middle of your country? Is it on a river/by the coast/in the mountains/on a lake or on a peninsula?
HISTORICAL INTEREST	Is your city important historically in any way? Can you name two famous people connected with your city? What are they famous for? When did they live?
LANDMARKS	Has it got any famous landmarks (places you can recognise from far away)?
SIGHTSEEING	Can you name: 2 religious buildings (church/ cathedral/mosque) 2 museums or art galleries 2 important government buildings 2 famous streets? (Why are they famous?) Is there anything else of interest for tourists – parks, sports centres, palaces, zoological or botanical gardens etc?
SHOPPING	Where is the best place to shop for (a) expensive clothes (b) cheap but fashionable clothes?
CUISINE	Is your city famous for any kind of food? Name some good restaurants.
TRANSPORT	What different means of public transport are there – tram, bus, underground, train, taxi?
CLIMATE	What's the average temperature in the middle of the hot season, and in the cold or rainy season? What sort of climate has it got – temperate (as in Europe), dry and hot (as in Egypt) or tropical (as in Malaya)?

Writing

Now write some short paragraphs describing your city or town. Use the text about Sydney on page 18 to help you.

📼 Listening

Listen to Sue and Paul describing their impressions of two capital cities, Moscow and Sydney. While you listen, note down what Sue thought about:

the climate in Moscow
the Red Square
the food

and what Paul thought about:

the climate in Sydney
the opera house
the food
the swimming

Oral exercises

1. Expressing geographical facts

I didn't realise that Mount Kilimanjaro was so high.
Yes, it's one of the highest mountains in the world, actually.

Heavens, did you know that the Amazon was over 3,000 miles long.
Yes, it's one of the longest rivers in the world, actually.

I didn't know Borneo was so large.
Is Lake Victoria really so big?
I didn't know it rained so much in Hawaii.
Is Death Valley really as hot as they say?

2. Describing features of cars

We definitely want a car that's economical on petrol.
Well, here's one which is economical on petrol.

And I think it should have back seat safety belts.
Well, here's one which has back seat safety belts.

Mm. It's got to be small and easy to park.
Perhaps it would be good to have an automatic gear-box.
It must have a folding back seat, of course.
Mm, well it must be reasonable in price.

3. Commenting on food and drink (Open exercise)

Use a suitable word: spicy/strong/sweet/cold/hot/cooked

How's the chicken?
I'm afraid it's not quite (spicy) enough for me.

Is the curry OK for you?
I'm afraid it's not quite (hot) enough for me.

Is the coffee all right?
How's the lager?
Is that tea all right for you?
How are you enjoying your hamburger?

4. Getting ready for a party

I'm worried there are too few chairs.
Too few? I think there are too many.

And I think there's too little to drink.
Too little? I think there's too much.

Aren't there too many glasses?
Isn't there too much rice salad?
I'm worried there are too few disco dancing records.
And, the other thing, I think there are too many girls coming.

5. Commenting on people's qualities

Look at the staff employment officer's notes.

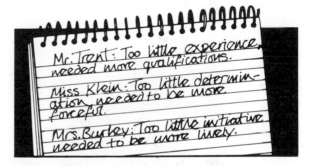

Mr. Trent: Too little experience, needed more qualifications.

Miss Klein: Too little determination, needed to be more forceful.

Mrs. Burkey: Too little initiative, needed to be more lively.

What did you think of Mr Trent?
I felt he didn't have enough experience.

Really?
Yes, he really wasn't qualified enough.

6. Confirming impressions

Did you read the Iris Murdoch novel I gave you? I thought it was fascinating.
Yes, it's one of the most fascinating books I've ever read, in fact.

Did you see that interesting film about Yugoslavia last night?
Yes, it's one of the most interesting films I've ever seen, in fact.

So you went to Crete, did you? It's a beautiful island, isn't it?
Did you hear Jack tell that funny story about his neighbour's cat?
You've also been to the Natural History Museum, haven't you. I thought it was fascinating.
I must say I thought that meal we had last night was delicious.

Unit 3   Richard gets a new job

Richard goes for an interview at AM-ADMEL and sees Mr Preston, the Sales Manager.

MR PRESTON: So you've had previous experience in selling, I see.

RICHARD: Yes, I was a representative for BSB, the office equipment people.

MR PRESTON: Oh yes. I know them. Well, we're looking for someone with ambition and initiative. Someone who's good at dealing with people and able to make new contacts.

RICHARD: Yes, I realise that.

MR PRESTON: So really, though the hours can be fairly flexible, you have to be prepared to work hard at this job. Perhaps harder than you imagine.

RICHARD: Yes. Well, I'm prepared to do that.

MR PRESTON: Oh . . . just a routine question. You can drive, can't you, and you have a current driving licence?

RICHARD: Oh yes.

MR PRESTON: Good.

Check

What experience has Richard had of selling?
What personal qualities is Mr Preston looking for?
What other qualification is necessary for the job?

📼 Listen and answer

What question did Mr Preston ask before he started to talk about the job?
Why do you think he asked that?
What reason did Richard give for wanting to leave his previous job?
Why is this job attractive to Richard?

Discuss

Do you think Richard has a good chance of getting the job?
What other qualities do you think are important if you want to be a successful sales representative?
Have you ever been for an interview?
What do you remember about it?

Set 1 Qualities and skills

1. Game: What's my job?

Divide yourselves into groups of about 6–8. One of you should think of a job and the others in the group must try to guess what the job is by asking questions about it. You may only ask questions which have a 'Yes' or 'No' answer. Below are a set of questions to start the game off, but you will need to ask other ones as well. Ask one question each so that everyone asks the same number of questions.

In your job …

Do you work …
inside?
outside?
in an office?
at home?
in a large building?
at weekends?
in the evenings?
shift hours?

Do you have to …
talk a lot?
meet a lot of people?
have special qualifications or training?
speak a foreign language?
give orders to others?

Do you …
travel?
drive?
wear a uniform?
work with your hands?
use any sort of tool?
use any sort of machine?
make or build anything?
type as part of your job?

Do you have to be …
imaginative?
ambitious?
attractive?

How many questions did you need to ask before you could guess the job?

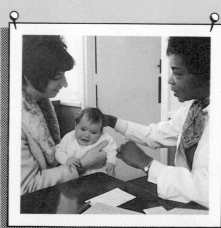

Unit 3

2. In pairs, think about what these jobs involve:

a secretary/personal assistant
a travelling sales representative
a language teacher
a tourist guide in London
a district nurse
an accountant

Now discuss each job under the following headings. Use the words and phrases suggested. Make notes as you discuss.

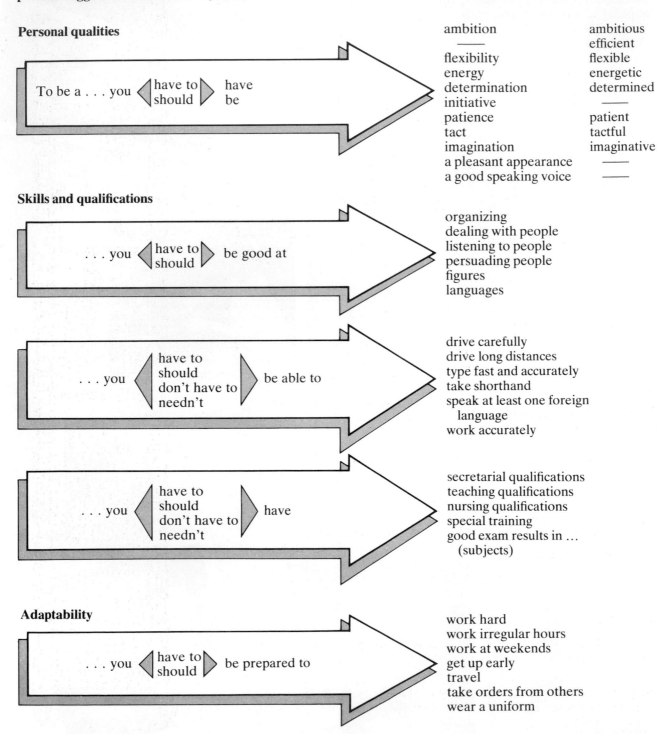

Personal qualities

To be a . . . you ◁ have to / should ▷ have / be

ambition	ambitious
———	efficient
flexibility	flexible
energy	energetic
determination	determined
initiative	———
patience	patient
tact	tactful
imagination	imaginative
a pleasant appearance	———
a good speaking voice	———

Skills and qualifications

. . . you ◁ have to / should ▷ be good at

organizing
dealing with people
listening to people
persuading people
figures
languages

. . . you ◁ have to / should / don't have to / needn't ▷ be able to

drive carefully
drive long distances
type fast and accurately
take shorthand
speak at least one foreign language
work accurately

. . . you ◁ have to / should / don't have to / needn't ▷ have

secretarial qualifications
teaching qualifications
nursing qualifications
special training
good exam results in ... (subjects)

Adaptability

. . . you ◁ have to / should ▷ be prepared to

work hard
work irregular hours
work at weekends
get up early
travel
take orders from others
wear a uniform

24

Set 2 Comparison

1. Notice these ways of comparing features of jobs.

Being a secretary | is much more / is just as / isn't as | interesting | than / as / as | being a typist

A teacher | is much better / is just as well / isn't as badly | paid | than / as / as | a nurse

A nurse's working day is | much longer than / just as long as / not as long as | a doctor's

The prospects | are better / are just as good / aren't as good | in law | than / as / as | in accountancy

A typist has to | work harder / type faster | than a secretary

Make as many statements as you can from the tables. Say only what you think is true. Refer to different jobs if you like.

2. In groups of three or four, compare:

either   a dentist and a doctor's profession
or   being self-employed and being employed by a company.

Think of the following:

pay, hours, prospects, training, holidays, job satisfaction

3. Roleplay

In pairs. Each of you must think about your own job (or one you know something about). Think about the pay, the hours, the prospects and so on.

Imagine that your partner is thinking of changing jobs. Try to persuade him/her that your sort of job is better than the one which he/she is doing at the moment.

Development

Heroes

(adapted from an article by Simon Walsh for 'Jobs Weekly Ltd')

'I think you're heroes coming out in all this,' said the woman. The 'hero' is Jim Charvill, a milkman from Unigate. 'All this' is the cold and wet morning on which Jim was doing his milkround.

The job is more complicated than people think. It involves more than delivering milk. Said Jim, 'Nowadays it's cream, yoghurt, fruit juice, eggs and bread too. And you've got to be good at book-keeping because you have to enter in the books each item you deliver to each house – and I have about 460 houses! Of course you have to be able to get on with people too.'

Jim thinks that one of the main advantages of being a milkman is going out on your own. It gives you a feeling of independence. And there is also the incentive of commission on top of your basic wage.

One disadvantage, of course, is the very early morning. Jim has to be at the depot at 6.30 every morning. But he finishes for the day at 1 p.m. However, most people still need milk at weekends and Jim feels that people in their mid-twenties and upwards are more suited to the job than young people, who prefer to have their weekends free.

In a few words, if you are an independent sort of person, if you are prepared to take on responsibility and if you are good at dealing with people, it could be the job for you.

Check

Why did the woman think that the milkmen were heroes?

What sort of things do milkmen deliver to houses?

Why is this complicated for a milkman?

What personal qualities does Jim think are important?

What are three advantages of being a milkman?

Are there any disadvantages?

Why does Jim think the job is more suitable for people in their mid twenties and over?

The last paragraph summarises the article. What three points does it make?

Find where these three points were mentioned in the text.

Writing

Make notes on the article under these headings:

A Milkman's Job
Duties:
Skills:
Personal qualities:
Advantages of job:
Disadvantages of job:
Most suitable age:

Isabel's colleague, John, at work in the classroom.

🔘 Listening

Listen to this teacher of children aged 5–7 comparing her job with that of a teacher in a secondary school (children aged 12–16). As you listen, note down the answers to these questions:

Does she like her job?
How long has she been teaching young children?
What sort of personal qualities does she think are needed?
What sort of skills and qualifications are needed?
Does she think that teaching older children is more interesting?
How does she think a junior school teacher compares with being a secondary school teacher?
How do their salaries compare?
What about the career prospects?
What sort of people does she think tend to become junior teachers?

Writing

Choose one of the jobs you discussed on page 24 or any other job that you are familiar with (e.g. your own if you have one). First arrange your notes under topic headings, like this:

Name of job:
Duties involved: i . . . .
                            ii . . . .
Personal qualities: . . . .
Skills and qualifications: i . . . .
                            ii . . . .
Advantages of job: i . . . .
                            ii . . . .
Disadvantages of job: i . . . .
                            ii . . . .

Now write three short paragraphs describing the job you have chosen. Decide how you are going to divide the headings into paragraphs first. You can start your composition like this:

A …'s job involves …ing … and …ing … To be a good …, you have to be/have …

Oral exercises

1. Stating personal qualities

Well, this man may be suitable for the job. But is he ambitious enough?
Yes, he certainly seems to have plenty of ambition.

And imaginative?
Yes, he certainly seems to have plenty of imagination.

Mm. He's got to be energetic too. Is he?
And is he determined enough, do you think?
And tactful too?
And really we need a flexible sort of person. Do you think he is?

2. Questioning skills

A primary school teacher is a very all-round sort of person, you know. You have to be able to sing, for example.
But you don't have to be that good at singing, surely?

Quite good, anyway. And you have to be able to play the piano.
But you don't have to be that good at playing the piano, surely?

And you have to be able to draw.
And also you should be able to paint.
And you need to act as well.
You should be able to play the guitar.

3. Stating job requirements

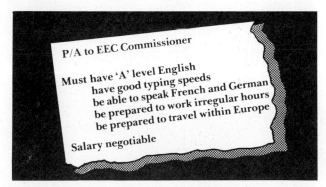

P/A to EEC Commissioner

Must have 'A' level English
have good typing speeds
be able to speak French and German
be prepared to work irregular hours
be prepared to travel within Europe

Salary negotiable

Here's a nice job – personal assistant to EEC Commissioner.

What does it say about qualifications?
It says you have to have 'A' level English.

Anything else?
It says you have to have good typing speeds.

I see. What about languages?

Really? And what about hours?
And I suppose it involves travelling?

4. Stating useful skills

Do I have to learn to type?
No, you don't have to, but typing's always useful.

Do I have to learn French?
No, you don't have to, but French is always useful.

Do I have to learn shorthand?
Do I have to have a car?
Do I have to go on a training course first?
Do I have to give a reference?

5. Making comparisons (1)

Well, how do you like nursing?
Well, to be honest, being a nurse isn't as interesting as I thought.

How are you getting on in your new secretarial job?
Well, to be honest, being a secretary isn't as interesting as I thought.

How do you find teaching?
What do you think of accountancy, then?
Do you enjoy hairdressing?
So you like the carpentry trade, do you?

6. Making comparisons (2)

A typist is talking to her friend at work.

The new girl is getting a rise in salary!
Really? why?

Because she types very well.
Well, I think you type better than her.

But she types fast, too.
Well, I think you type faster than her.

The thing is, she works so fast.
Mm, and of course, she dresses well.

Unit 4 Richard remembers

Richard has now settled into his new house and new job. One evening he invites Gill, a friendly girl from work, to have a meal with him at home. They chat after supper.

GILL: You've got a lot of Abba records!

RICHARD: Yes, my wife used to be very keen on them at one time.

GILL: What happened to your wife, Richard?

RICHARD: She died in a car accident.

GILL: Oh, I'm sorry.

RICHARD: It's all right. I don't mind talking about it now.

GILL: How long ago did it happen?

RICHARD: Last summer. It happened while she was driving home from work.

GILL: How long were you married?

RICHARD: Seven years. We got married as soon as she left college. I was only twenty. It seems such a long time ago. So much has happened since then.

Check

Why does Richard have a large collection of Abba records?
How did his wife die?
When did it happen?
When did they get married?
How long were they married?

Listen and answer

What did Richard do soon after his wife's death?
Why did he move to Wimbledon?

Discuss

Do you think Gill is:
– just being polite to Richard
– being sympathetic and kind
– being rude and inquisitive?

Past time: remembering facts and habits

> My wife used to be keen on Abba.
> She didn't use to like jazz very much.
> Where did you use to live as a child?

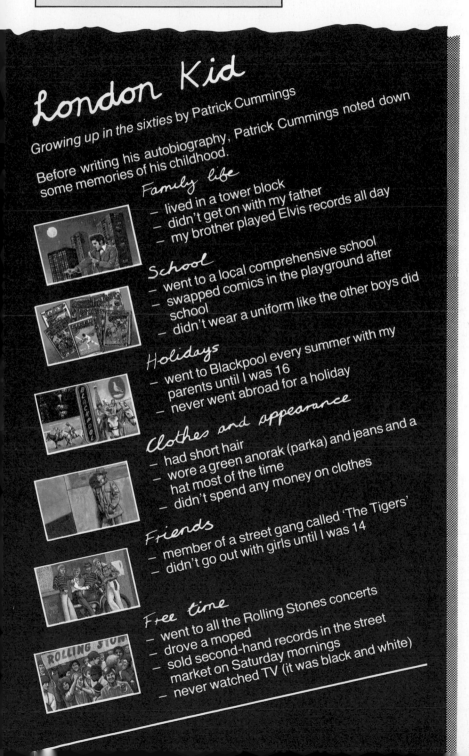

London Kid

Growing up in the sixties by Patrick Cummings

Before writing his autobiography, Patrick Cummings noted down some memories of his childhood.

Family life
- lived in a tower block
- didn't get on with my father
- my brother played Elvis records all day

School
- went to a local comprehensive school
- swapped comics in the playground after school
- didn't wear a uniform like the other boys did

Holidays
- went to Blackpool every summer with my parents until I was 16
- never went abroad for a holiday

Clothes and appearance
- had short hair
- wore a green anorak (parka) and jeans and a hat most of the time
- didn't spend any money on clothes

Friends
- member of a street gang called 'The Tigers'
- didn't go out with girls until I was 14

Free time
- went to all the Rolling Stones concerts
- drove a moped
- sold second-hand records in the street market on Saturday mornings
- never watched TV (it was black and white)

1. **In pairs, talk about Patrick Cummings' memories, like this:**

> What
> Where did he use to …?
> How

What sort of … did he use to …?
What does he remember about …?

He used to …
He didn't use to …
He never used to …

2. **Note down some of your own memories of your past. Use the same headings as here to help you remember. Then ask your partner to recall some of his or her memories.**

Unit 4

Past time: point and duration

TWICKENHAM HIGH SCHO
SCHOOL LEAVERS 1972

Angela Bartlett (1968–72)
Marion Carew (1966–72)
Karin Dewhurst (1967–72)
Gillian Ferguson (1968–72)
Teresa Framley (1969–72)

POINT OF TIME

She left secondary school: *at the age of* 16
in 1972
8 years *ago*
when she was 16
as soon as she got her O levels
after she got her O levels
before she was 17

DURATION

She worked in a hospital: *during* her school holidays
for a few months
until she *went* abroad
while she *was* still *studying* at school

She's been working here: *for* a year
since last year
since 1979

CHANGE OF ADDRESS
Mr and Mrs Ferguson are
moving from Ham, Surrey
to
33 St Margarets Close
Twickenham, Middlesex.
on July 20th 1968

1. Write as many sentences as you can about your own life up till now using suitable time expressions from the list above.

Now ask your partner about his or her past life. Help by asking questions like:

What did you do | when / before / after | you ...?

How long did you ...?

How long were you | in / at | ...?

What were you doing while you were ...?
How long have you been ...?

2. Study these pieces of information about Gill's early life and then listen to Gill talking to Richard about her more recent life. Make notes about what she did and when.

3. Now ask your partner:

– when Gill was born
– how old she was when she started school
– when her parents moved to Twickenham
– how long she was at Twickenham High School
– how old she was when she left school
– what she did during her school holidays
– what she did as soon as she left school
– how long she was there
– when she did her secretarial course
– when she got the job in the travel agency
– how long she worked there
– when she got the job at ...
– how long she has been working there.

4. Fill in the missing words in the following paragraph about Gill's early life.

Gill was born ... 1956. She started at Ham First School ... ... of five. ... she was twelve, her parents moved to Twickenham. She went to Twickenham High School ... she was sixteen. ... she was in her last year at school, she worked in a hospital ... the holidays.

Now continue: ... she left school, she ...

Now write another similar paragraph about Gill's recent life using your notes and the answers to the questions in exercise 2.

5. Write two paragraphs about your own past life, using suitable time expressions to link your sentences.

DK 627743
[Printed b

CERTIFIED COPY of an ENTRY OF BIRTH.
Pursuant to the Births and Deaths Registration Act, 1953.

Registration District   SURREY NORTH EASTERN
Sub-district of   MERTON AND CARSHALTON   in the   COUNTY OF SURREY

May 12th, 1956	Gillian Anne	John Mary Jane		Ferguson

Registrar of Births and Deaths for the Sub-district of MERTON AND CARSHALTON , in the COUNTY OF SURREY   *See note overleaf.*
copy of the entry No. 316 in the Register of Births for the said Sub-district, and that such Register is now legally in my custody.
MY HAND this 24th day of May 19 56
the particulars on this
is true, knowing it to
Registrar of Births and Deaths.

Development
Marilyn Monroe

Year	Age	Event
1926	0	At 9.30 a.m. on June 1st Norma Jean Mortensen was born in Los Angeles General Hospital. At the age of six months, Norma Jean was placed with foster parents.
1933	7	Norma Jean went back to live with her mother. She went to school at the Hollywood Grammar School.
1934	8	Norma Jean's mother became ill. The doctors diagnosed her as insane and she entered Los Angeles State Mental Asylum. Some English neighbours offered to look after the child.
1935	9	The English couple could no longer take care of Norma Jean. She went into an orphanage in Los Angeles and stayed there for two years.
1937	11	Norma Jean left the orphanage and went to the first of a series of temporary families.
1942	16	She left school. On June 18th, three weeks after her sixteenth birthday, she married an 18-year-old young man whose name was Jim Dougherty.
1944	18	Norma Jean got a job as a parachute packer with the Radio Plane Company. While she was working, a photographer used her as a model for a magazine article. The photographer persuaded her to take a part-time course in modelling. Norma Jean left her job at the Radio Plane Company and became a full-time photographic model. Soon she appeared on several national magazines and calendars.
1946	20	Norma Jean wrote to her husband, who was stationed in the navy in Shanghai, to say that she wanted a divorce.

Check

When was Norma Jean born?
Who did she spend the first six months of her life with?
After returning to her mother, why did she only stay with her for a year?
Who offered to look after Norma Jean?
Where did she go after that? Why?
Where did she live after the age of eleven?
When did she get married? To whom?
What was her first job?
What other work did she do during this period?
How did she become a full-time photographic model?
When did she decide to divorce her husband?

Writing

Look back at the account of Marilyn Monroe's early life. In what ways was her childhood miserable? Write a short paragraph to support this statement. Start like this:

'I do not imagine that Marilyn Monroe's childhood was a happy one. As soon as she was born, she was placed with ....'

On July 16th, 1946, Norma Jean Dougherty went to Twentieth Century Fox studios without an appointment and asked to see Ben Lyon, the casting director for Fox films. Lyon agreed to see her.

'What can I do for you?' Lyon asked.

'I want more than anything to get into pictures,' she said. Lyon looked at her.

'Honey,' he told her, 'you're *in* pictures.'

He immediately offered her a seven-year contract starting at 75 dollars a week. During the next 16 years Marilyn Monroe made over thirty films and remarried twice.

On Saturday, August 4th, 1962, she took an overdose of sleeping pills and died. She was just thirty-six.

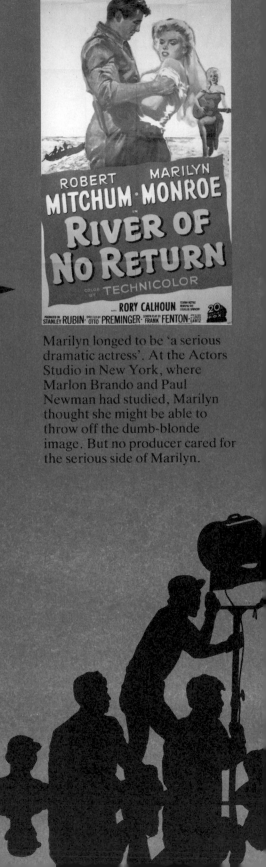

Marilyn longed to be 'a serious dramatic actress'. At the Actors Studio in New York, where Marlon Brando and Paul Newman had studied, Marilyn thought she might be able to throw off the dumb-blonde image. But no producer cared for the serious side of Marilyn.

Billy Wilder describes the back seat of her black Cadillac: 'There's blouses lying there and slacks, dresses, old shoes, old plane tickets … you never saw such a filthy mess in your whole life. On top of the mess is a pile of traffic tickets. . . . Is she worried about this? Am I worried about the sun rising tomorrow?' (Norman Mailer: *Marilyn*)

'Marilyn loved animals, in fact she loved all living things. Once she spent hundreds of dollars to try and save a tree damaged by a storm. She used to make tree-houses for birds and give them food and worry about them when the weather was bad.' (Norman Rosten: *Marilyn – An Untold Story*)

Check

The different texts on these pages show many different sides of Marilyn Monroe's personality. Which texts or part of a text support the view that Marilyn was:

(a) kind and gentle
(b) attractive and photogenic
(c) untidy and careless
(d) unhappy when she died?
(e) ambitious and had initiative
(f) unhappy about her image?

📼 Listening

Listen to Sue and Paul telling stories about their fathers. Try to suggest which personal characteristic(s) the stories reveal.

Writing

Write a few paragraphs about someone you remember well from your childhood or your past. It could be a member of your family, a teacher, a very good friend, your first boy/girl friend…

Try and write three paragraphs. Think of what you are going to say in each paragraph first. You may like to discuss it with your partner before you start writing.

Look at this guide first:

Paragraph 1:
Who is the person? Is it a relation or a friend? If it isn't a member of your family, how did you get to know him/her? How often did you use to meet?

Paragraph 2:
Why did he/she make an impression on you? What special qualities did he/she have? Can you remember any stories which illustrated these qualities – anything he/she used to say/do/wear and so on?

Paragraph 3:
What has happened to this person since then? Perhaps you haven't seen him/her for a long time? Why? When did you last meet?

Start like this:

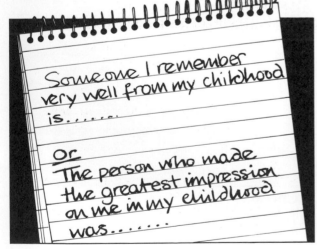

Someone I remember very well from my childhood is…….

or
The person who made the greatest impression on me in my childhood was…….

Oral exercises

1. Expressing point of time

Look at Norma Jean's biography on page 33.

When was Norma Jean placed with foster parents?
In 1926, at the age of six months.

When did she go back to live with her mother?
In 1933, at the age of seven.

When did she go to stay with the English neighbours?
When did she enter the orphanage?
When did she leave the orphanage?
When did she get married?

2. Expressing duration

Look at page 33 again.

How long did Norma Jean stay with her foster parents?
For six and a half years, until she was seven.

How long did she stay with her mother?
For a year, until she was eight.

How long did she stay with the English neighbours?
How long did she stay at the orphanage?
How long did she stay at school?
How long was she married to Jim Dougherty?

3. Asking for details about the past (1)

I left school in 1962.

What did you do after you left school?
I got some secretarial qualifications.

What did you do after you got your qualifications?
I took an office job but left after six months.

I spent a year abroad.
I did a nursing course and passed my exams in 1968.
Well, then I got married and had a baby.
I returned to work after a year or so, and I've been at this hospital since 1972.

4. Asking for details about the past (2)

When I left school I was unemployed.

What did you live on while you were unemployed?
I got social security money. Then I travelled round Europe for a bit.

What did you live on while you were travelling round Europe?
Oh, I got odd jobs. Then I did voluntary work in Africa for a year.

Well, they paid me something. Then I went back and started studying.
I got a grant. Then I did a course.
Oh, it wasn't too bad. I managed.
But then I gave it up and wrote a novel.
I borrowed some money. And now I'm going to America.

5. Remembering past facts and habits

You are at a party.

Meet John. He teaches at the High School.
How funny! I used to teach at the High School too.

And this is Sandy. She lives in Wembley.
How funny! I used to live in Wembley too.

And this is Mark. Mark has just got an old black Volkswagen.
And you must meet Lucy. Lucy, that's a wonderful dress! Lucy buys all her clothes from street markets.
Oh, let me introduce you to Clive. Clive's at Kent University. He's reading History.
Well, you seem to have lots in common with everybody, so I'll leave you to enjoy yourself.

6. Questioning people's past habits

A friend of yours has become health conscious.

I don't smoke any more now, you know.
Oh, did you use to smoke a lot, then?

Quite a lot, yes. And I don't eat any more sweet things.
Oh, did you use to eat a lot of sweet things, then?

Yes, and I don't drink any more now.

Oh, quite a bit. And I never drive anywhere, you know.
Yes, too much. The marvellous thing is that I don't feel tired any more now.
Yes always. And I'm never ill any more either.
Mm, often. I feel a new person!

Learning checklist

In these units you have learnt how to:

Unit 1

1. Describe people using a relative pronoun 'who' 'whose'

   I have a brother
   – who lives in Libya
   – whose main interest is collecting old cars.

2. Describe places using relative 'where'

   There's a good school where he can send Kevin.

3. Express purpose using a purpose clause with 'to'

   I'm saving money to go to America.

4. Express purpose using a purpose clause with 'so that'

   I'm lending my sister some money so that she can go to college.

Unit 2

1. Describe places using 'there is' 'have got'

   There's a good school down the road.
   We've got a small garden.

2. Describe features of places using the relative 'which'

   We've got a small garden which is a bit untidy.
   There's a theatre which people say is very good.

3. Describe features of places using the superlative adjective '-est' or the superlative 'most' + adjective

   It's the prettiest town I've ever seen.
   It's one of the most interesting places I've ever been to.

Unit 3

1. Talk about qualities and skills using
    'should'/'have to'/'don't have to'
    + 'have'   You should have imagination.
    + 'be'   You should be efficient.
    + 'be able to'   You don't have to be able to take shorthand.
    + 'be prepared to'   You have to be prepared to work irregular hours.

2. Talk about qualifications and skills using   You have to have special secretarial qualifications.
    'have to' + 'have'

3. Compare features of jobs using the   A secretarial job is
    comparative form
    adjective + '-er' + 'than'   – better than …
    'more' + adjective + 'than'   – more interesting than …
    'as' + adjective + 'as'   – just as boring as …
    'not as' + adjective + 'as'   – not as well paid as …
    adverb + 'er' + 'than'   You have to work harder than …

Unit 4

1. Express past time in sequence using
    'while'   While I was working in France, I lived in a hostel.
    'as soon as'   As soon as I left school, I got a job.
    'during'   During the war, we lived in the country.
    'before', 'after', 'since'

2. Recall memories using 'used to'   We used to go to Brighton for our holiday.
                                                 I remember my brother used to work in a café.
                                                 I never used to like school.

NATIONAL UNION OF
JOURNALISTS
7 John Street, Bedford Row, London, W.C.I
'Phone :   Telegrams :
HOLborn 2258   Natujay Holb, London

This is to certify that

Mr. GEORGE ORWELL
of The Tribune

is a member of the   T. + P.
Branch of the National Union of Journalists.
Leslie R. Aldous   Branch Sec.
(Address) 66, Priory Gdns., N.6.
                                    Member's Sig.

George Orwell

1. Look at the words printed in *italics*. Write down the names of the newspapers and magazine mentioned in the text.

2. Which are Orwell's two most famous books?

3. Work out, with dates, Orwell's:
– journalistic career
– literary career
– other periods of employment or service.

4. Make out a full 'curriculum vitae' for George Orwell.

5. What did you learn about Orwell's life that:
– most surprised you
– most interested you?

6. Many of Orwell's books have a political slant to them. Which parts of his life do you think influenced his political views?

Write about the life of a friend or a member of your family that you know well.
Try and use these words:

when	while	as soon as	after
before	during	until	
at the age of	in	for	since

About the author . . . .

Eric Arthur Blair (George Orwell) was born in 1903 in India, where his father worked for the Civil Service. The family moved to England in 1907 and in 1917 Orwell entered Eton, where he contributed regularly to the various college magazines. He left in 1921 and joined the Indian Imperial Police in Burma the following year, in which he served until 1928.

His first published article appeared in *Le Monde* in October 1928, while Orwell was living in Paris, and he returned to England in 1929 to take up work as a private tutor and later as a schoolteacher (1932). *Down and Out in Paris and London* was published in 1933. Due to his poor health, Orwell gave up teaching and worked as a part-time assistant in a Hampstead bookshop, and later was able to earn his living reviewing novels for the *New English Weekly*, a post he kept until 1940.

At the end of 1936 Orwell went to Spain to fight for the Republicans and was wounded. During the Second World War he was a member of the Home Guard and worked for the BBC Eastern Service from 1940 to 1943. As literary editor of *Tribune* he contributed a regular page of political and literary commentary. From 1945 Orwell was the *Observer's* war correspondent and later became a regular contributor to the *Manchester Evening News*.

Orwell suffered from tuberculosis, and was in and out of hospital from 1947 until his death in 1950. He was forty-six.

His publications include *The Road to Wigan Pier, Coming up for Air, Keep the Aspidistra Flying* and *Homage to Catalonia*. Orwell's name became widely known with the publication of *Animal Farm* and *Nineteen Eighty-Four*, both of which have sold more than two-million copies.

Possible aims for secondary schools

Which five aims do you think are most important for a secondary school?

- to help you do as well as possible in examinations.

- to teach you about different sorts of jobs and careers so that you can decide what you want to do.

- to teach you things that will be useful in running a home; for example, how to bring up children, home repairs, decorating.

- to help you to learn how to get on with other people; such as, those you work with, your future wife or husband.

- to teach you to speak well and clearly.

- to teach you to be able to write easily.

- to help you to become independent and able to stand on your own feet.

- to help you develop your own personality and character.

- to teach you what is right and wrong.

- to help you to know what is going on in the world nowadays.

- to teach you plenty of subjects so that you can be interested in lots of things.

1. Work in pairs. Read out your list of aims to each other, like this:

I think the most important aims are to …, to …

**2. Question each other's choice.
Here are some ways you can do this:**

– I think it's [more / just as] important to … [than / as] to …

or
– I still think the most important aim is to …
or
– Why is it important to …?
– Well, so that they can …

3. Write down any other important aims you can think of and discuss them with the class.

4. Think of your own schooldays, or think of what schools and education were like twenty years ago.

What sort of things did you/children use to learn?
What did they use to think were the most important aims of education? Is it any different now?
Which subjects did you use to enjoy?

Match the following famous people with a description of who they were and what they did. Make lists in your notebook and draw arrows between the correct pieces of information.

Buddy Holly	English scientist	lived in Stratford upon Avon
Abraham Lincoln	pilot	painted the ceiling of the Sistine Chapel
Michelangelo	English political reformer	died in a plane accident
Shakespeare	famous pop singer	famous for his theory of evolution
Charles Darwin	famous sculptor	flew the Atlantic alone
Amy Johnson	American president	campaigned for votes for women
Emmeline Pankhurst	English playwright	was shot in a theatre

Now make full sentences about each of these people using 'who', **like this:**

Buddy Holly was a famous pop singer who died in a plane accident.

Ludwig van Beethoven (1770–1827)

Beethoven was one of the greatest composers the world has known. He was a master at expressing his feelings through symphonies and choral music. He composed his greatest works in a short period between 1805–8. He is best remembered for his nine symphonies of which the *Pastoral* and *Eroica* are the most popular.

Now choose some people to talk and write about from the following list:

a novelist	an architect
a film star	a politician
a painter	a film director
a scientist	a poet
a sportsman or woman	a sculptor
an actor or actress	a pop group

Were they great, beautiful, important, influential, exciting, controversial?

In pairs, discuss your choice first, like this:

– Let's choose …
– Really? I think … is more well-known.
– But he's not as influential as …
– I disagree. I think he was just as influential as ….

Choose at least three or four to write about. Use the following model to help you.

(Picasso) was one of the (greatest and most influential painters) of this (century). (He) is best remembered/most well-known for (founding Cubism). One of (his) most popular/famous/well-known (paintings) is (*Guernica*).

Read your paragraphs out to the rest of the class. Discuss each others' opinions, like this:

I don't think Picasso's most popular painting was *Guernica*. I think it was *Les Demoiselles d'Avignon*.

It is said that in the sixth century, one thousand years before Columbus, Saint Brendan, a great Irish missionary, made a voyage from Ireland to America in a leather boat. On May 17th 1976, Tim Severin and his crew of four, set off from Ireland in a similarly constructed leather boat to see if such a journey was possible. Thirteen months later they reached the New World. In his book, *The Brendan Voyage*, Tim Severin writes about their living conditions:

'The shelter inside the cabin measured no larger than a big double bed. Somehow we had to find enough room for three people to sleep, plus their clothing, a radio telephone and all the camera and navigation equipment.
Each of us knew that we were all living together under very raw conditions. We were like men locked in a small cell. The scope for argument was limitless. We all adopted a 'live-and-let-live' attitude and kept ourselves to ourselves.'

NOTICE

As you may know, the college of Education runs a series of short summer courses for foreigners (aged 14-18) in July and August every year. Unfortunately the college hostel is too small to accommodate all the students and we usually try to place some of them with families who live within a reasonable distance of the college.

If you feel you have suitable facilities and would like to take in a paying guest for part of the summer, could you please contact Mrs Chapman, at the College of Education.

The Spastic Society runs residential homes, as well as hostels, schools, job-training centres and workshops for the spastics. A spastic has cerebral palsy, which means that the part of the brain which controls movement does not work properly. A spastic often speaks unintelligibly and is unable to make a co-ordinated movement. A volunteer with time and patience can sometimes help these spastics. It is not easy. I once went to a residential home for spastics and listened with them to a talk by an outside speaker. One of the symptoms of cerebral palsy is that when a person is excited or interested, his arms and legs can move in violent spasms. The talk was an interesting one, and there were spasms. After the talk, many wanted to ask questions. But it can take minutes for a spastic to form one sentence. The speaker listened to each question very calmly, always waiting until the full question was formed. I don't think I could have done it. And this kind of volunteer work may not be for you.

Read the texts and, in groups, discuss the personal qualities, skills and qualifications needed to:

either   (a)   join the crew of a boat like *Brendan* crossing the Atlantic.

or   (b)   become a volunteer in a spastics residential home.

or   (c)   live in a strange family as a foreign guest.

Try to use these expressions:

| You should You have to | be able to ... have ... be prepared to ... | because ... |

Present your points to the other groups afterwards.

Sandy

'Who am I? Well, I'm 22. My full name is Sandra Alison Bates but people call me Sandy. I live with a girl called Val in a flat in Wembley. I chose Wembley because it's near my job. I work as a programme assistant for LTV, the TV company. Well, I'm *called* a programme assistant but I'm really a secretary. I type, file letters and make tea for my boss. My boss is a woman, by the way. I thought my job was going to be really interesting. I've always wanted to work in the media but I'm a bit disillusioned now: My boyfriend, Mark, also works there. He's a video technician.

I don't see so much of the rest of my family now. My mum and dad live in Wandsworth, in South London and I'm in Wembley so it's a bit far away. My younger brother, Dave, still lives with them but he and I don't get on very well. Richard's all right. He's my older brother. He's just moved to Wimbledon with his kid, Kevin. I sometimes go and babysit for him. I like Kevin. He's good fun.'

Check

What do you know about Sandy? (name, age, where she lives, her job)
What does she think of her job?
What contact does she have with the rest of her family?
How does she get on with them?

Unit 6 Sandy makes arrangements

Sandy is working in her office at LTV. Something has gone wrong with the video recorder in the office and she telephones her friend, Mark, who works as a technician in the maintenance department. She asks him to come and look at it.

SANDY: Oh Mark?... Sandy here... Look I'm afraid there's something wrong with the office video... Oh, I don't know. The picture is wobbly. Do you think you could come and look at it?... Yes, I suppose so. I'm only typing a letter... I'll see you in a few minutes then.

A few minutes later, Mark arrives.

SANDY: Oh hi! There's the video over there.
MARK: Look, I'm afraid I haven't got time to fix it now after all. I'm doing something in Studio 14 at 11 o'clock. But I'll be free at 12. I'll do it for you then. OK?
SANDY: Fine. I'll be here all morning.
MARK: Look, if I can't come at 12, I'll get someone else to fix it.

Stella, a senior programme assistant, enters.

STELLA: Sandra, would you mind finishing those letters please. They are important, you know.
SANDY: Yes, Stella.

Check

Where is Sandy?
What does Mark do?
Why does Sandy telephone Mark?
What is wrong with the office video?
Why can't he fix it immediately?
When will he be able to do it?
What will Mark do if he can't come at 12?
What does Stella ask Sandy to do when she comes into the office?

🔲 Listen and answer

Who is Sandy typing a letter to?
How do you know from their conversation that Sandy and Mark know each other outside work?
How does Stella behave towards Sandy?
What does Sandy think of Stella?

Discuss

What do you think Mark said to Sandy on the phone?
What were his actual words?
What do you do if something goes wrong with your television at home?
Do you think a video recorder for the home is a useful present?

46

Polite requests

Polite and friendly
Do you think you could come and look at it?

Polite but formal
Would you mind signing your name here please?

---

1. In pairs, practise making the two different types of requests.

Informally to a friend:
you think the TV is on too loud
you want a lift to the station
you want the window open a little
you want your letter posted

Formally to a stranger:
you would like him/her to move his/her car
you would like him/her to sign the visitor's book
you want to know the way to the main entrance of a building
you want a passer-by to be a witness to a car accident you have just had.

2. Make requests to suit the following situations. Act the situations in class.

You and a friend are on a train and you need help in lifting your suitcase down from the rack.

You would like the garage attendant to check the oil level in your car.

You and your mother are shopping and you need her help to open the car door as you have a lot to carry.

You are in a bank and you would like to change a £10 note.

You are in a café and you would like the person sitting next to you to lend you his/her newspaper so you can check the cinema times.

You have been to a friend's house for the evening and you want your friend to telephone your husband/wife/mother to say that you are on your way back.

Future arrangements and predictions

I'm doing something in Studio 14 at 11 o'clock.
I'll be free at 12.
I won't be free until 12.

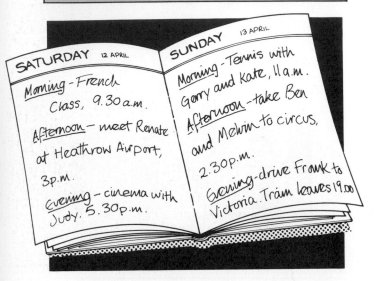

SATURDAY 12 APRIL

Morning – French Class, 9.30 a.m.

Afternoon – meet Renate at Heathrow Airport, 3 p.m.

Evening – cinema with Judy, 5.30 p.m.

SUNDAY 13 APRIL

Morning – Tennis with Gerry and Kate, 11 a.m.

Afternoon – take Ben and Melvin to circus, 2.30 p.m.

Evening – drive Frank to Victoria. Train leaves 19.00

1. Use the diary entries above to practise conversations, like this:

– Do you think you could come over on Saturday morning?
– Well, I'm going to a French class at 9.30 but I'll be back by 11 o'clock. Is that all right?
– What about meeting on Saturday afternoon?
– I'm afraid I can't. I'm meeting Renate at Heathrow at 3 o'clock and I won't be back until about 5.

2. Note down your own arrangements for:
this evening
next Saturday
next Sunday

Invite your partner to join you where suitable, like this:

– I'm … this evening. Would you like to come too?
– I'd love to. I'm not doing anything special myself.
or
– I'm afraid I can't. I'm … and I won't be back until …

3. Roleplay in groups of five or six.

You work in business and you are having a meeting.
You want to fix a date for another meeting during the following week.

Draw a diary in your notebooks and mark Monday to Friday. Write down the following engagements, placing them on any of the five days and at any time between 9 a.m. and 5 p.m.

going to a reception (say where)
meeting a foreign visitor (say whom)
going to a meeting (say which)
doing a press interview (say for which newspaper)
taking the morning/afternoon off (say why)
visiting a factory (say which)

One of you is the chairperson of the meeting. He/she must try and arrange a time to suit each individual in the group.

Set 3

Offers and promises

> I'll fix it for you at 12.
> If I can't come then, I'll get someone else to fix it.

1. After a party at a friend's house....
In groups, sort out how you can offer to help your friend clear up, like this:

I'll put the records back in their covers for you.

This is the situation:
– there are a lot of dirty glasses and dirty plates
– the ashtrays are full of cigarette ends
– the air in the room is unpleasant
– the furniture is in another room
– there is a lot of rubbish and empty bottles in the kitchen
– there are a lot of crumbs on the carpet
– records are lying about without their covers.

2. In pairs, use the frames below to make different conversations, like this:

– You won't forget to come on Saturday evening, will you?
– No, but if I can't make it, I'll let you know.
– Yes, do that because if you don't, I'll wonder what's happening.

A You won't forget to | come on Saturday evening / pick me up from the station on Sunday / write that letter to the bank | will you?

B No, but if | I can't make it / I can't do it / I'm away / I haven't got the time | I'll | let you know / give you a ring / ask someone else to do it

A OK, fine

3. Roleplay

You	Your friend
Explain to a friend that you are having difficulty putting some bookshelves up	Offer to help
Suggest a convenient time	Apologise and say you're busy. Say what you're doing then and when you'll be back
Suggest an alternative time	Agree and promise to contact your friend if your plans change

Development

The slow train to China

Angela Singer reports at the start of a very unusual trip.

John and Dorothy Shackleton-Bailey were two travellers not surprised by the announcement at Victoria Station, London, yesterday.

'Will passengers for Paris, Berlin, Warsaw, Moscow, Irkutsk, Peking, Nanking, Shanghai, Canton and Hong Kong please go to platform one.'

The travellers were boarding the Central Kingdom Express and pioneering a 14,930 km (9,331-mile), 42-day rail link between London and Hong Kong. Next year the service will be a monthly feature.

Mrs Shackleton-Bailey, aged 73, from Blockley, Gloucestershire, is the oldest in the party organised

by Sunquest Holidays. 'It's no good sitting back if you retire. One must do things one hadn't time to do before, and the people who want to do a trip like this will be interesting, don't you think?'

The youngest is 33-year-old Mrs Ildi Moran, who will be leaving husband Mike Moran working at their house in Radlett, Hertfordshire.

The trip will end with a direct return flight from Hong

Kong and will cost each traveller almost £1,800. 'I decided to go as soon as I saw the advert,' said 68-year-old Mr Denis Haviland of Hampstead, London. 'I've always wanted to see China and I started life as a railway-man, so I don't mind spending six weeks on trains.'

Mr David Barber, a stamp dealer, and his wife, Jeannine, from Hungerford, decided in October to take a trip. 'We wanted to go straightaway to see

China and to eat Chinese food, which we love.'

The courier, Prue Stern, who is going to stay with the group all the way, said, 'I don't think there will be any problems. The job involved lots of planning and detailed arrangements. We are picking up the final member of the party in Paris.'

Check

Where are the people travelling to?
How are they travelling?
How long will the trip take?
What countries are they going to pass through?
What is the age range of the travellers?
How much does the trip cost each person?
Why do the Shackleton-Baileys want to go?
Why won't Mr Haviland mind spending so long on a train?
Why are the Barbers looking forward to arriving?

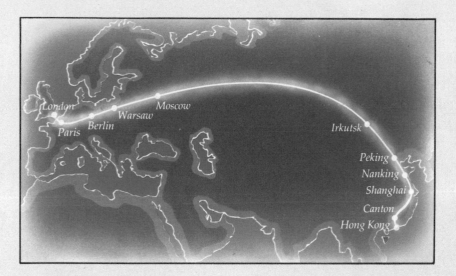

3. Make a list of the advantages and disadvantages of going on a trip like this.

4. Roleplay. Imagine that you very much want to go on this trip. You try to persuade a friend to join you. Your friend is not so sure about it. Use your notes from exercises 2 and 3 to help you in your arguments.

5. Have you got any plans for a long trip or holiday like this in the near future? If so, tell the rest of your group about them.

1. Follow on the map the route the train is going to take.

2. In pairs, discuss what the travellers can do at each stop, like this:

If they have any time in Paris,

they	can	see	…
	ought to	go to	
		do	

Roleplay

You are having trouble with your car. A friend of yours from work is a mechanic and has promised to come and have a look at it.

– You both work until five thirty.
– You think the job will take about one or two hours.

Telephone and ask if he/she can come over soon. Arrange a time.

Writing

You are going to spend your next summer holiday touring Britain by car. A friend has recommended a hotel in York where you would like to spend a few days. Write a letter to the manager of the hotel asking him to reserve you a room (or rooms). Before you write decide:

i.   what date you are arriving in York
ii. how many nights you are staying
iii. how many of you there are (only you or your family too?)
iv. what sort of room(s) you would like (single/double with shower or bath?)

Start your letter like this:

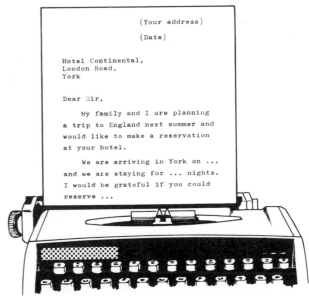

```
                    (Your address)

                    (Date)

Hotel Continental,
London Road,
York

Dear Sir,

    My family and I are planning
a trip to England next summer and
would like to make a reservation
at your hotel.

    We are arriving in York on ...
and we are staying for ... nights.
I would be grateful if you could
reserve ...
```

End your letter Yours faithfully, **followed by your signature. Print your name in brackets underneath it.**

🎧 Listening

Listen to Rod talking about his plans for the coming week. Write down his plans for each day.

Oral exercises

1. Polite requests: formal and informal

Ask a stranger to help you push your car.
Would you mind helping me push my car?

Ask a friend to lend you five pounds.
Do you think you could lend me five pounds?

Ask a friend to give you a lift to the airport.
Ask your bank manager to send you a new cheque book.
Ask a policeman to direct you to the motorway.
Ask a friend to feed your cat while you are away.

2. Stating arrangements

When are you going to see your parents again?
I'm seeing them this Friday, actually.

It's a long time since you've been to the theatre, isn't it?
I'm going this Friday, actually.

When are you going to meet the new director, Mr Barnes?
You need to see the doctor about that cough.
You must go to the exhibition at the National Gallery.
Why don't you take Sally to the children's theatre?

3. Stating definite times (1)

You have a number of things to collect this week. Look at the list.

When can I collect the photographs?
They'll be ready by Tuesday.

What about the cleaning?
It'll be ready by Wednesday.

Tuesday - Photographs
Wednesday - Cleaning
Friday - Shoes
Next Monday - Coat
Thursday evening - Car
Next Saturday - Picture

4. Stating definite times (2)

Use the same information to respond like this:

When can I collect the photographs?
I'm afraid they won't be ready until Tuesday.

When can I collect the cleaning?
I'm afraid it won't be ready until Wednesday.

5. Offering help

You and a friend are going on a long holiday.

Goodness, I must telephone the Embassy about the visas.
I'll telephone them for you.

Oh, thanks. And then there are the travellers cheques to collect.
I'll collect them for you.

Will you? Thanks. And I must fetch the tickets too.
Oh, thank you. And I mustn't forget to buy a new film for my camera.
Thanks. Oh yes. There are the suitcases to get down from the attic.
Oh, would you? I must go to the chemist's, you see.
Oh, you *are* kind. Now what am *I* going to do?

6. Checking arrangements

I'll meet you at the airport.
Well, if you can't meet me, will you let me know?

I'll come to the meeting, don't worry.
Well, if you can't come, will you let me know?

I'll fetch the children from school, don't worry.
Don't worry, I'll give you a lift tomorrow morning.
Don't worry, I'll return those library books for you.
I'll find his address, don't you worry.

Unit 7 Sandy wants a change

NOTICE TO ALL STAFF AT LTV   **IMPORTANT**

Due to the recent government financial cuts, we have been forced to make the following changes:

Meals & light
refreshments: The canteen will only be open for meals between
                    12-2pm and 6-8pm. It will not be open in the
                    morning or afternoon. Coffee and tea will be
                    available from the automatic machines.

Telephone calls: All outside telephone calls must go through the
                    switchboard.

Heating: The central heating system will only operate
                    between October 1st and April 30th and will
                    have a constant temperature of 66°F (19°C).

Travel expenses: If you wish to reclaim travel expenses, you
                    must fill in a claim form, attach a receipt
                    and state the purpose of the journey.

Check
Why are LTV making some changes?
When will the canteen now be open?
Where will staff be able to buy their tea and coffee?
Can they still make outside calls on the telephone?
When will the central heating operate?
What temperature will it be at?
What must staff do if they want to reclaim their travel
  expenses?

Sandy has just arrived at Richard's house to babysit for Kevin. She is talking to Richard about the financial cuts at LTV.

SANDY: And they're being mean about the heating
           too. They're only going to have it at 66
           degrees all through the winter. If it's a
           long hard winter like last year, nobody
           will come in to work. We'll have a strike.
RICHARD: But they've got to save money somehow,
           Sandy.
SANDY: Look! There are hundreds of ways of
           saving money. Do you know, if I wanted
           to make cuts, I'd stop all those expense
           account lunches at Mama Roma's. And
           I'd make the management staff come in
           before ten o'clock!
RICHARD: Well, I'd raise the whole thing at a union
           meeting if I were you.
SANDY: I think I will. But they never listen to us
           junior staff. Honestly, if I could find a
           better job, I'd leave tomorrow.
RICHARD: Would you really, Sandy?
SANDY: Yes, I would.

Listen and answer:
Why has Sandy gone to see Richard?
Why is she late?
What sort of mood is she in? Why?
Why does Richard advise her to leave her job?
What two changes does Sandy complain about?
Is Richard sympathetic?
How does Sandy say that she would save money if she
  had the chance?
What does Richard suggest she does?

Discuss
Do you think the changes are sensible?
What other ways of saving money in a large company
  can you think of?

Set 1 Advice and consequences

> If I were you, I'd leave.
> If I were you, I wouldn't leave just yet.

1. You have a visitor from abroad. Give advice about:

where to stay (somewhere fairly inexpensive)
where to eat local food at a reasonable price
what to buy as a souvenir or something typical of your
  country
what local sights to see
how to get to a place of interest
what books to read in your language

In groups of three discuss like this:
– Where do you think I should stay?
– If I were you I'd stay at …
– Oh, no, I wouldn't stay there, it's too close to the
  station. I'd stay at …, if I were you.

Start your questions like this:

Where	
When	do you think I should …?
What	
How	

> If they take the coast road,
>   they won't get there before dark.
>   they may not get there before dark.
> If they take the motorway, they'll get there sooner.

2. The Robinson family – Clive and Anne, Clive's mother and their two children aged 5 and 3 – are driving to southern Italy for a holiday in a rented villa just outside Salerno.

They have reached Naples and it is early afternoon. There are two routes to Salerno: the coast road via Sorrento, one of the most spectacular coastlines in the world, and the motorway – a shorter and more direct route.

Clive and his mother have always wanted to see the Amalfi coast. It is a hot but exceptionally clear day.

Anne has been keeping the children amused all the morning in the back of the car …

Work out the consequences of taking the coast road, like this:

If they take the coast road	they may run out of petrol
	it'll take them much longer

> If I were you, I'd go to Bristol. It would definitely be cheaper.
> But it might be boring.
> It wouldn't be boring at all. There's plenty to do in Bristol.

3. Helena is a Polish girl who wants to go to Britain to study for a year. She has two important decisions to make: where to go and where to live.

Look at the different possibilities within each decision. Then look at the advantages and disadvantages of each possibility.

DECISION 1

Where to go	Advantages	Disadvantages
London	more to see and do more language schools to choose from	lonely too many distractions expensive
Bristol	cheaper easier to find somewhere to live more of the country to see	not as exciting as London
A seaside town	near the sea easier to meet people plenty to do in the summer	full of foreign students lots of old people boring in winter cold

DECISION 2

Where to live	Advantages	Disadvantages
With a family as paying guest	company of other people no cooking or cleaning opportunity to speak English all the time	expensive may not get on with family
With a family as 'au pair'	company and opportunity to speak English earn some money	not enough time to study not always free in the evenings no private life
In a hostel or bedsitter	free to do whatever she likes cheap accommodation	lonely not very comfortable
In a shared flat	company of people of same age complete freedom	expensive housework to do difficult to study

Helena asks a friend for advice. In pairs, act out the conversation between them. Discuss the advantages and disadvantages of each decision.

Start like this:
– Where do you think I should go?
– Well, if you went to London, there'd be more to see and do.
– But it would be expensive of course.
– Yes, and it might be lonely. On the other hand, there'd be more language schools to choose from.

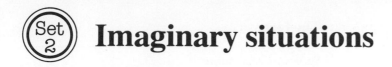

Imaginary situations

> If I found £5 in the street, I'd give it to the police.

1. Make up a personality quiz for a magazine.
In pairs or groups think of three questions for each section and write them down.
Then choose somebody else in the class to answer the questions.

WHAT WOULD YOU DO? FIND OUT WHAT SORT OF PERSON YOU ARE

ARE YOU HONEST?	If you found £5 on the street	(a) .... (b) .... (c) ....
	Your friend has bought a new coat which you don't like. If he asked you for your opinion	(a) .... (b) .... (c) ....
ARE YOU PRACTICAL?	If you saw an accident in the street	(a) .... (b) .... (c) ....
	If you woke up in the night and saw your curtains on fire	(a) .... (b) .... (c) ....
	If you arrived at the airport to go on holiday and found that you didn't have your passport	(a) .... (b) .... (c) ....
ARE YOU IMAGINATIVE?	If you won £1000	(a) .... (b) .... (c) ....
	If you could take a year off work	(a) .... (b) .... (c) ....

2. In groups, discuss any measures you would take if you were Minister for:

Education   Social Services   the Environment   Finance   Foreign Affairs   **in your country.**

Development

Benfield's million

The background

Benfield is a small suburban town in North London. It is fairly densely populated. There is a small residential area on the outskirts of the town but most people live close to the centre on housing estates or in small terraced houses. Although there are some local industries, many people commute to London to work.

The town has little to offer in terms of sports or cultural facilities, and very few open spaces.

Recently an ex-MP for Benfield died, leaving the town £1 million to be spent on a 'living monument which will be beneficial to the community'.

There is an area of uncultivated land on the outskirts of the town, quite close to a school, on which the council could get permission to build if necessary. The local council have called a meeting to decide how to spend the money most usefully.

The facts

Sport and recreation

The only sport catered for in Benfield is football. There is an area on the common which schools use and which the public can use at other times. None of the schools has a swimming pool. The nearest public pool is in the neighbouring town, Fleetwood, 5 km (3 miles) away. Fleetwood Comprehensive School has an athletics track which Benfield schools can use once a week in the spring and summer terms. There are no parks for old people to enjoy and few children's playgrounds.

Culture and entertainment

Vandalism among young people is a serious problem for the police in Benfield. Many say that it occurs because there is not enough for young people to do in their spare time. There is one cinema which is old and in need of repair. The council have been thinking of spending money on improving it, or closing it down altogether. Anyone who wants to go to the theatre, a concert or an art gallery, has to travel up to London. The bus and train service is not very reliable and the last trains and buses leave London at 11.30 p.m. There is nowhere for old people to meet. The nearest library is in Fleetwood 5 km (3 miles) away.

Environment

Benfield is situated very close to a large ring road round North London, used especially by heavy lorries. People who live close to it are always complaining about the noise of traffic and the smell of the fumes. Because of the lack of real open spaces and natural scenery in Benfield, people find it difficult to get away from the smoke-filled atmosphere and traffic which is typical of a suburban town close to London.

Read the facts about Benfield. Divide yourselves into groups of four or five. Discuss how you think you could use the money most usefully. Think of all the facilities that are lacking in Benfield. What sort of 'living monument' could you build?

The pictures on this page may give you some idea of the sort of suggestions you could make, like this:

If we build a library, they won't need to go to Fleetwood.
If we had a sports centre, everyone would be able to use it.

Try to use some of these expressions in your discussion:

Giving an opinion
In my opinion …
If you want my opinion …

Agreeing
I agree (with …)
I think … is right.
That's exactly what I feel.

Disagreeing
I'm afraid I don't agree (with …)
I don't think you're right.
Yes, but listen …
That's nonsense!

Interrupting to make a point
Forgive me for interrupting but …
Can I say something?
Can I make a point?

Summarising
Can we agree then that …
Shall we say then that …
Well, it seems that the best solution is to …

🔊 Listening

Several people were asked to say what they would do in certain situations. Listen and write down the questions you think they were asked, like this.

(a) What would you do if …?
(b)
(c)

Writing

Either

Write a paragraph saying what you would do if you could take a year off to do exactly what you liked with no children or relatives with you and no real money problems.

or

Write a letter to a friend who is thinking of coming to Britain to study for a year. Recommend places to go and where to live. Give reasons for your suggestions.

Oral exercises

1. Giving advice with a reason (Open exercise)

I thought I'd buy a motorbike.
Really? I wouldn't buy a motorbike if I were you. (They're very dangerous.)

We're thinking of going by car to Scotland.
Really? I wouldn't go by car if I were you. (Petrol is so expensive nowadays.)

We might move to London, actually.
I think I'll go and see *Dracula* this evening.
We're thinking of going to Spain for our summer holidays.

2. Giving reasons for buying a bicycle

So you think I should buy a bicycle, not a car?
Yes, you'll save a lot of money.

Really?
Yes, and you'll keep fit.

3. Explaining consequences to children (Open exercise)

Why must I brush my teeth?
Well, if you don't brush your teeth, (you'll get toothache).

Why must I go to bed now?
Well, if you don't go to bed now, (you won't be able to get up in the morning).

Why must I eat vegetables every day?
Why must I go to school?
Why do you always have to go to work?
Why must I drink milk?

4. Disagreeing with plans

I'm going to give up my job.
I think you'd regret it if you gave up your job.

But I want to move to the country.
I think you'd regret it if you moved to the country.

I thought I'd sell my flat.
And I'd buy a little cottage.
I'd sell the car.
And I'd have the telephone removed.

5. Putting yourself in imaginary situations

I'd like to go to America.
Really? I wouldn't go to America if you paid me!

I might move to London soon.
Really? I wouldn't move to London if you paid me!

Mm. I'd quite like to go into politics.
I'm also thinking of taking up yoga.
I might go on a walking holiday next summer.
And I'm thinking of selling my car!

Unit 8 Sandy reports

Sandy is having lunch with her flat mate, Val, in a wine bar in Marylebone High Street. Sandy is talking about a recent interview with her boss, Stella.

VAL: Come on Sandy, tell me what she said.
SANDY: She said she was very disappointed in me.
VAL: No!

SANDY: Yes, she did. She said she didn't like my attitude. She said I was difficult to work with. And she said she wouldn't be able to give me promotion. She even asked if I had thought about getting another job.
VAL: But surely she can't give you the sack?
SANDY: No, she can't. Anyway, I told her I thought the work wasn't very interesting. Well, you know how boring it is.
VAL: What did she say to that?
SANDY: Well, I think she understood. She said she might be able to find me something different to do.
VAL: Like what?
SANDY: Testing audience reaction – you know, asking people if they like certain programmes.
VAL: Oh, well Sandy, cheer up. At least it will get you out of the office.

Check
What time of day is it?
Who is Val?
What are Sandy and Val talking about?
Who is Stella?
What did Stella say she didn't like about Sandy?
What did Sandy say about the job?
What did Stella say she might do?

🎧 Listen and answer
What did Stella want to talk about? Why?
Where did the meeting between Stella and Sandy take place?
What did Stella say about Sandy?
How did Sandy defend herself?
What did Stella say to make Sandy feel happier?

Discuss
How useful do you think this kind of interview is?
What do you think about Stella's way of talking to Sandy?
How would you describe Stella's attitude towards Sandy?

Set 1 **Reported requests**

Friendly and informal
'Do you think you could help me?'   She asked me to help her.
'Please don't tell anyone.'   She asked me not to tell anyone.

Polite and formal
'Would you mind signing your name please?'   He asked me to sign my name.
'Could you sign your name please?'

'Would you mind not smoking.'   She asked us not to smoke.
'I'd rather you didn't smoke.'

With authority

'Leave me alone!'   He told her to leave him alone.
'Don't move!'   He told us not to move.

1. Report the following requests:

'Would you mind opening your suitcase, please?'

'Please don't wake me before eight.'

' I'd rather you didn't pay by cheque.'

'Come on, move back. Move back there!'

'Do you think you could feed the cat today?'

'Don't make a sound!'

2. Say the actual words

The policeman asked me to spell my surname.
The teacher told the children to stop talking.
She asked her husband to lay the table.
The airsteward told them not to panic.
Her mother asked her not to be back late.
The tourist guide asked them not to leave anything valuable in the coach.

Set 2 **Reported statements**

AM – WAS	'I'm British,' he said.	He said (that) he was British.
ARE – WERE	'We're coming,' they said.	They said (that) they were coming.
HAVE – HAD	'I've finished,' she said.	She said (that) she had finished.
DON'T – DIDN'T	'I don't like tea,' she said.	She said (that) she didn't like tea.
LIKE – LIKED	'I like your room,' he said.	He said (that) he liked her room.
TOOK – HAD TAKEN	'I took the letters,' he said.	He said (that) he had taken the letters.
CAN – COULD	'I can't see him,' she said.	She said (that) she couldn't see him.
WILL – WOULD	'I'll come tomorrow,' he said.	He said (that) he would come tomorrow.
MAY – MIGHT	'It may rain,' she said.	She said (that) it might rain.

What they said about New York

A group of Europeans went on a ten-day visit to New York. It was the first time they had been there. They were interviewed during their stay.

'It's a perfect choice of holiday for anyone who likes bright lights and lots to do.'
Maria Pei from Italy

'It's not as expensive as I imagined. You can live here quite cheaply if you know the right places to go. Yesterday I had an excellent meal for 5 dollars.'
Nico Iannopolos from Greece

'I have never seen such a beautiful city in my life.'
Bruce Matlock from Bristol, England

'I love it. It's very noisy, very dirty but very full of life. I'll definitely come back next year. Ten days is too short.'
Etienne Matthieu from Paris, France

'I don't like New York at all. It's too impersonal. I may not stay here for the full ten days.'
Kersti Kristiansen from Denmark

'I've found the people very friendly and very generous. And there seems to be far more integration between black and white people than I imagined.'
Gilles Poitier from Luxembourg.

'We don't like the 'fast food' but the food you get in the restaurants is wonderful. You can get almost anything you like here.'
Martin Dressler from Germany

1. Report what each person said about New York.

2. Report in general what they said about:

the cost of living
entertainment
eating out
the people
New York life

oo **3.** **Listen to the conversation between Stella and Sandy. Match the actual words with the way in which Sandy reported them to her friend, Val, later. For example 1 = G**

1. 'Perhaps you need a change? Have you ever thought about working somewhere else?'	A She told me to meet her at 12.30.
2. 'Would you mind meeting me for lunch tomorrow?'	B She said I was 'difficult'.
3. 'Yes, I think I understand how you feel. I'm glad you told me.'	C She asked me to meet her in a little Italian restaurant.
4. 'I'm not very pleased with you. It's something about the way you approach your work. Your attitude to it.'	D I told her I thought the work wasn't very interesting.
5. 'Meet me there at 12.30, could you?'	E I think she understood.
6. 'I'm not going to beat about the bush. I'm going to be very frank with you.'	F She said she was disappointed in me and didn't like my attitude.
7. 'It's just that my job, what I do, seems so boring, so repetitive. I don't feel I'm getting anywhere.'	G She even asked if I had thought about getting another job.
8. 'Bill Fletcher who deals with audience reaction and research wants someone to help him out on door-to-door interviews and so on. We might be able to fit you in somewhere there.'	H She said she wouldn't be able to give me promotion.
9. 'I can't honestly recommend somebody for promotion who doesn't take an active interest in their work.'	I She told me she was going to be very frank.
10. 'In fact I find that you're not very easy to work with. Yes, really, Sandra I find you rather difficult.'	J She said she might be able to find me something different to do.

Reported Roulette

Work in pairs.
Either:
choose 5 questions to ask your partner
or:
ask your partner to choose 5 numbers between 1 and 14 on the roulette wheel and ask the questions which correspond to the numbers your partner has chosen.

Question your partner about his or her answers. Record your partner's answers and report them back to your group.

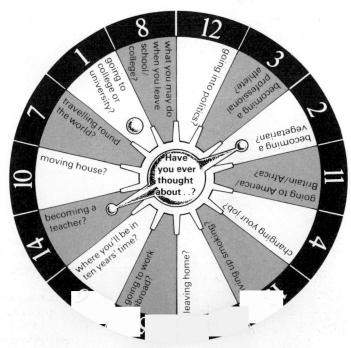

65

Development

What makes Eddie Kidd jump?

(based on an article by Mike Nicks in 'Bike' Feb. 78)

Eddie Kidd is a motorcycle stunt artist who wants to become the king of stunt motorbike riding. He is young, confident and brave; he is also hoping to earn £1,000,000 by doing dangerous stunts like jumping over 13 double-decker buses on his motorbike.

At 18, Eddie is Britain's answer to America's Evel Knievel, the man who tried and failed to 'shoot over' the Grand Canyon on a motorbike.

How does he compare himself with Evel Knievel. 'Evel knows how to make big money. I know how to make it too.'

Eddie knows what he's going to do with his money.

'I'll buy my own house with a lot of land so that I can do all my bike training at home. Then I'm going to have my own cinema, a little disco for my friends, a pinball machine and my own hamburger stand.'

How long will it take Eddie to earn his first million?

'It may take a couple of years. Then I'll be king of the stunt riders.'

Eddie made his first public jump at an air show when he was 15. He was with a team of riders called the Cyclomaniacs. Then, when he was 17 he jumped 13 double-decker buses.

Does he think the stunt was worth it?

'I'm still the only rider in the world who has jumped over double-decker buses. I only got £150 for doing that but I got a lot of publicity in the newspapers and on TV.'

What does Eddie do before he makes a jump?

'Well, I touch the back of the chain and wipe the grease from my glove on the back of my heel. I also say to myself, "God, get me over here please".'

But what about accidents? Surely it's only a matter of time before Eddie Kidd has a serious accident?

'I'm confident enough not to have accidents. I do enough training and physical exercises. I don't drink too much. My training consists of swimming, running and physical workouts. Normally I train every day, and I also train on the bike once or twice a week.'

It all sounds so easy. Aren't there any special skills or qualities that a stunt rider needs to have to be successful?

'I can't really explain these because I've been doing stunt riding since I was 13. Something just makes me do it. I don't know what it is.'

Perhaps it's just for the money?

'No, I don't jump or risk my life just for the money. I'm doing it because I like doing it and I want to be the best stunt rider in the world.'

Check

What questions did Mike Nicks ask Eddie Kidd?
What did Eddie say about money and how important it was to him?
What does he do immediately before each jump?
What did he say about his training schedule?
What did he say about his reasons for risking his life.?

Roleplay

Imagine that you go with Sandy to London Heathrow Airport to meet a television executive from Senegal, West Africa. Sandy has a letter from the executive, Mr Gaston Kaba, giving details of his arrival. You wait for an hour at the pre-arranged meeting point but Mr Kaba does not arrive. Use the letter below to check the travel arrangements with Sandy. Start like this:

YOU: Well, he's not here. Are you quite sure that he's coming today?

SANDY: Yes, he said he was definitely coming on Tuesday the 22nd.

Continue the conversation.

> 20 Rue de Denian,
> Dakar,
> Senegal
>
> Dear Miss Bates,
>   Thank you for your letter. I am definitely coming to London. The date you suggest suits me fine and I am arriving on Air France flight 252 (Terminal 2) at 5.30 on Tuesday October 22nd.
>
>   I will meet you by the Information Desk. I am flying from Dakar to Paris and I may have trouble with my connection. If I do, I can catch a later Air France flight which arrives at 6.45 p.m.
>
>   I have booked a hotel room at the Penta Hotel in Cromwell Road near the West London Air Terminal for four nights so if I miss you, I'll go straight there by airport coach. I hope nothing goes wrong with my travel arrangements because I have arranged to meet some friends from the BBC at 9.15 in the cocktail bar.
>
>   Looking forward to
>   meeting you,
>   Yours sincerely,
>   Gaston Kaba.

Listening

Listen to Evelyn talking to Paul about a recent trip she made to New York. Report her impressions of the following:
the people
the cost of living
the food
the night life and entertainment

Report Evelyn's impressions by writing a few sentences under each of the headings, like this:

The people
She said that the people were … but that she had only met …

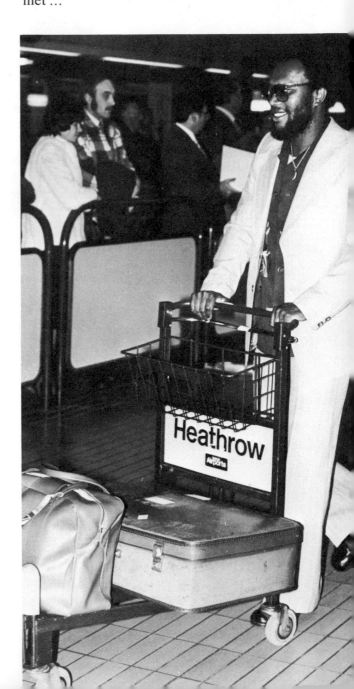

Oral exercises

1. Spot the clue!

A policeman is interviewing a man called Mr Forsythe who claims that one of his valuable paintings has been stolen. After the interview the policeman suspects that Mr Forsythe is not telling the truth. Spot the clue and find out why.

2. Reporting requests (1)

Your boss asks you to come and see him to talk about something confidential. You report to a friend afterwards what he asked you to do.

Come in please.
First he asked me to come in.

I'd rather you didn't tell anyone about this meeting.
Then he asked me not to tell anyone about the meeting.

Would you mind closing the door.
And would you mind not talking too loudly.
Do sit down.
Now could you please tell me what you know about the new plans.

3. Reporting requests (2)

A teacher is taking his pupils round a museum. Before they go, he asks them to repeat the rules he has given them.

Now what did I tell you first?
You told us to meet at the entrance at ten o'clock.

What else?
You told us not to touch anything.

```
Here are the rules:

Meet at the entrance at 10 o'clock
Don't touch anything.
Take notes as you look at everything.
Don't talk too loudly.
Don't leave the rest of the group.
Keep well together.
```

4. Reporting people's actions and experiences

Some overseas students are visiting your town for the first time. A friend asks how their visit is going.

Have they been to the museum yet?
Yes, they said they'd been there.

Did they enjoy it?
Yes, they said they'd enjoyed it.

Have they seen the art exhibition?
Did they like it?
Have they tried any local food?
Have they visited the market yet?

5. Reporting a meeting

You attended a meeting at work which your friend was unable to come to. Report what Mr Barker, the sales manager, said.

MR BARKER: 'I talked to Mr Jones the other day. He's done all the research. But I'm not happy about the price. It all sounds too expensive. I'm trying to reduce it slightly and I'll let you know if it's possible.'

Well, what happened at the meeting?
Well, Mr Barker said he'd talked to Mr Jones the other day.

And?
He said he'd done all the research.

What about the price?
Why?
So what's he going to do?
Do you think he can?

Unit 9 Sandy investigates

Sandy is doing a questionnaire for LTV to test the public's interest in sports programmes.

▣ Listen and answer

Listen to Sandy's interview with a member of the public whom she called on one afternoon.

Write down his name, age and his answers as you listen.

What sort of questionnaire is Sandy doing? Why?

Would you say that Tony was very interested in sport? Give reasons for your answers.

Discuss

Do you watch sports programmes on television?

What are your favourite sports?

Do you think there should be more sport on television?

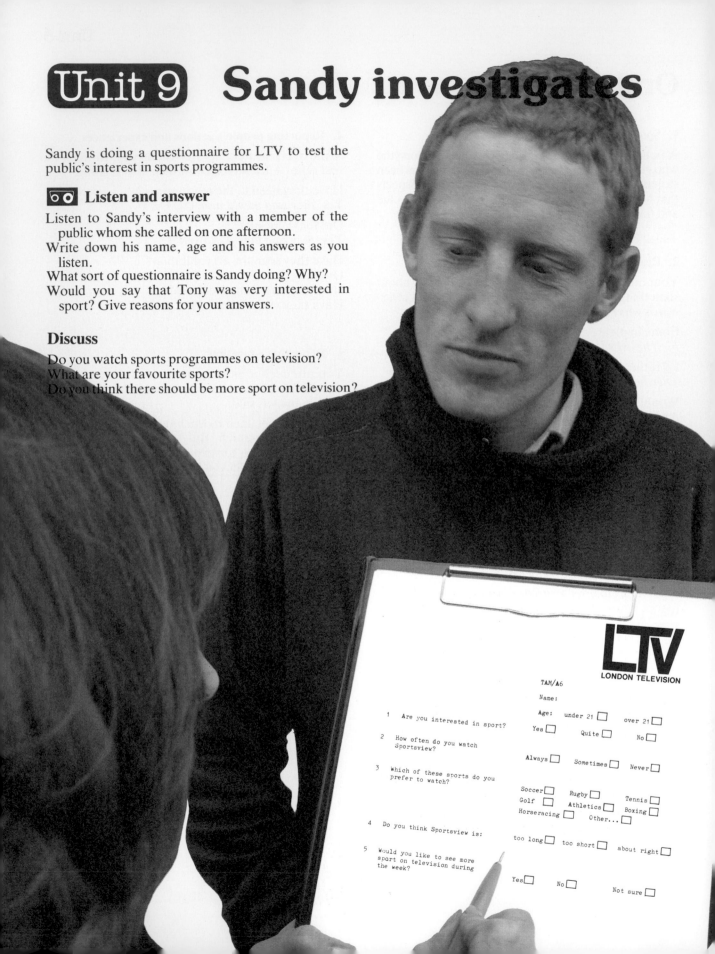

LTV
LONDON TELEVISION

TAM/A6

Name:

1 Are you interested in sport?

2 How often do you watch Sportsview?

3 Which of these sports do you prefer to watch?

4 Do you think Sportsview is:

5 Would you like to see more sport on television during the week?

Age: under 21 ☐   over 21 ☐
Yes ☐   Quite ☐   No ☐

Always ☐   Sometimes ☐   Never ☐

Soccer ☐   Rugby ☐   Tennis ☐
Golf ☐   Athletics ☐   Boxing ☐
Horseracing ☐   Other... ☐

too long ☐   too short ☐   about right ☐

Yes ☐   No ☐   Not sure ☐

Set 1 Reported questions

How old are you? ... She asked me how old I was.
Are you over 21? ... She asked me if I was over 21.

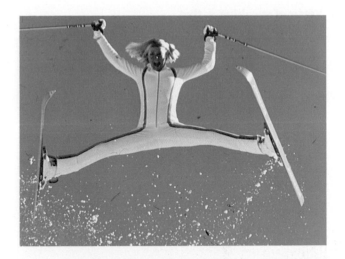

1. Tony Collins tells a friend of his, Anna, about the questionnaire. He tells her the questions which Sandy asked him. Fill in his part of the following conversation with Anna.

TONY: She asked me questions about sport on TV.
ANNA: What sort of questions?
TONY: Well, first she asked my name, and then she asked me if I ...
ANNA: I wonder why she wanted to know that. Go on.
TONY: Then she asked ...
ANNA: So you said yes.
TONY: No, I said I was *quite* interested. So then she asked how ...
ANNA: You watch it all the time, if you ask me.
TONY: No I don't. I said sometimes. Then, let's think. Oh yes, she asked ... and she listed a whole lot.
ANNA: I can guess. You said soccer.
TONY: Yes, and athletics. Let's see. Then she asked ...
ANNA: I hope you said it was too long.
TONY: I can't remember. Then she asked ...
ANNA: And you said?
TONY: I said 'No'. And that was it.
ANNA: Mm. You feel important now, don't you?

When you have completed the conversation, read it with your partner.

2. Write down six questions to ask your partner, starting with:

Are you ...? Have you ever ...? Did you ...? How often do you ...? Where ...? What ...?

In pairs, ask and answer the questions. Note down the questions your partner asked you.

Then form new pairs. Report the questions which your first partner asked you, and your answers.

Reported speech and behaviour

Verbs of speaking + that

SAY	
'It's hot.'	He said (that) it was hot.
AGREE	
'Yes, it *is* hot.'	He agreed (that) it was hot.
EXPLAIN	
'I've been out in the sun and I'm hot.'	He explained that he was hot.
REPLY	
(Can you come?) 'No, I'm afraid I'm busy.'	He replied that he was busy
COMPLAIN	
'This food is cold!'	He complained that the food was cold.
SUGGEST	
'Let's go.'	He suggested (that) they went.
But notice	
TELL	
'You're wrong!'	He told **me** (that) I was wrong.

Verbs of speaking + pronoun + to + verb

ASK	
'Would you mind signing this?'	He asked me to sign it.
TELL	
'Come in and shut the door.'	He told me to come in and shut the door.

Verbs of speaking + to + verb

OFFER	
'Would you like me to take you?'	He offered to take me.
REFUSE	
'Sorry, but I won't do it.'	He refused to do it.
AGREE	
'OK I'll do it for you.'	He agreed to do it for me.
But notice	
APOLOGISE	
'I'm sorry I broke the vase.'	He apologised **for breaking** the vase.

1. Change the following from direct to reported speech. Use he or she.

'Why don't we all go out and have something to eat?'
'Well, you see, I always oversleep in the morning.'
'It's a really exciting film.'
'But the beaches are *always* dirty in the summer.'
'You're right. I *do* get angry very quickly.'
'No, I can't help you with your homework.'
'Yes, the summers are very hot in Egypt.'
'What about having a Fancy Dress party?'
'The trouble is that my bed is uncomfortable.'
'You're a liar!'
'Yes, I think Dave is a bit thoughtless, too.'
'I posted the letter last week.'

2. Match the following verbs of speaking with the actual spoken words. Then report the speech, like this:

He refused to …

REFUSE	'I'm sorry I hurt your feelings.'
OFFER	'Look! I said I am *not* going to the party.'
APOLOGISE	'Give me the facts! You must give me the facts!'
ASK	'Would you like something nice and cold to drink?'
PROMISE	'Right. I'll be secretary of the meeting.'
AGREE	'Trust me. I won't say a word to anyone.'
TELL	'Could you give me a ring tomorrow?'

3. Write the following paragraph as a conversation between Dave and Carol.

Dave rang Carol at work and apologised for not phoning her earlier. He told her that he had tickets for a concert on Saturday. She agreed to go and he offered to pick her up at 6.15.

Verbs of speaking + noun/pronoun

INTRODUCE	
'Peggy, meet Barry.'	She introduced Peggy to Barry.
GREET	
'Hello everyone, nice to see you.'	She greeted everyone.
ACCEPT	
'All right, I'll take the money.'	She accepted the money.
REFUSE	
'No thanks, I don't drink.'	She refused a drink.
EXPLAIN	
'My difficulty is I can't see too well at the back of the classroom.'	She explained her difficulty.
INTERRUPT	
'But listen Barry, (could I just say something about this?)	She interrupted Barry.

4. In pairs, create appropriate situations and ...

introduce someone
greet and reply to a greeting
offer and accept something
offer and refuse something
explain a problem, a reason or a difficulty
interrupt someone

5. Report each stage of the following conversation in separate sentences.

MARJORIE: Well, I'm off to the meeting now, Stanley.
STANLEY: Really? But you're always going out to meetings.
MARJORIE: I know, but this one's very important.
STANLEY: What time does it finish?
MARJORIE: About nine o'clock, I think.
STANLEY: Well, would you like me to pick you up in the car afterwards?
MARJORIE: Yes, that would be lovely.
STANLEY: All right, then. I'll meet you outside the Town Hall just after nine.
MARJORIE: You won't forget, will you?
STANLEY: No, I promise I won't.

6. Listen to the tape and imitate the intonation.

'Why are you always late!' she said angrily.
'No I won't,' he said rudely.
'No I won't, he said politely.
'No, no, not now,' she said quickly.
'Come and have some tea,' said the old lady in a friendly voice.

7. Try saying the following in the ways suggested:

'*It's the police.*' – slowly
– nervously
– quickly
– in a friendly voice
– in a frightened voice

'*Pass the butter, would you.*' – politely
– rudely
– quietly
– timidly

'*This is how you do it.*' – patiently
– impatiently
– sarcastically
– decisively

Development

Death on the Nile

Agatha Christie is known throughout the world as the Queen of Crime. Her seventy-seven detective novels and books of stories have been translated into every major language, and her sales are calculated in tens of millions.

She began writing at the end of the First World War, when she created Hercule Poirot, the little Belgian detective with the egg-shaped head and the passion for order – the most popular detective in fiction since Sherlock Holmes. Poirot, Miss Marple and her other detectives have appeared in the many films, radio programmes and stage plays based on her books. Agatha Christie died in 1976.

Death on the Nile

Linnet Ridgeway is the young and beautiful heiress to an immense fortune, but she has a lot of enemies. One of the people who hates her is Jacqueline (Jackie) de Bellefont whose handsome fiancé, Simon Doyle, she has stolen and married. Jackie jealously follows the newly-wed couple on their honeymoon trip to Egypt.

At Luxor a party of people, including Hercule Poirot, prepare for a trip up the Nile on the river steamer the *Karnak*. Poirot senses the tension between Jackie, Linnet and Simon. Just before the trip he warns them to be careful.

The *Karnak* anchors at Abu Simbel. The passengers go to bed ready for another day's sightseeing of the magnificent temples.

Next morning Linnet is found dead in her cabin with a bullet hole in her head. Someone has shot her at close range. Then there is another murder, and then another. There is death on the Nile. Hercule Poirot has to solve another baffling mystery …

This extract takes place before the trip on the Karnak. *Poirot is talking to Simon about Jackie.*

'There is nothing, then, of the old feeling left?'
'My dear Monsieur Poirot – how can I put it? It's like the moon when the sun comes out. You don't know it's there any more. When once I'd met Linnet – Jackie didn't exist.'
'Tiens, c'est drôle, ça!' muttered Poirot.
'I beg your pardon.'
'Your simile interested me, that is all.'
Again flushing, Simon said: 'I suppose Jackie told you that I'd only married Linnet for her money? Well, that's a damned lie! I wouldn't marry any woman for money! What Jackie doesn't understand is that it's difficult for a fellow when – when – a woman cares for him as she cared for me.'
'Ah?' Poirot looked up sharply.
Simon blundered on: 'It – it – sounds a caddish thing to say, but Jackie was *too* fond of me!'
'Une qui aime et un qui se laisse aimer,' murmured Poirot.
'Eh? What's that you say? You see, a man doesn't want to feel that a woman cares more for him than he does for her.' His voice grew warm as he went on. 'He doesn't want to feel *owned*, body and soul. It's that damned *possessive* attitude! This man is *mine* – he *belongs* to me! That's the sort of thing I can't stick – no man could stick! He wants to get away – to get free. He wants to own his woman; he doesn't want *her* to own *him*.' He broke off, and with fingers that trembled slightly he lit a cigarette.
Poirot said: 'And it is like that that you felt with Mademoiselle Jacqueline?'
'Eh?' Simon started and then admitted: 'Er – yes – well, yes, as a matter of fact I did. She doesn't realise that, of course. And it's not the sort of thing I could ever tell her. But I *was* feeling restless – and then I met Linnet, and she just swept me off my feet! I'd never seen anything so lovely. It was all so amazing. Everyone kowtowing to her – and then her singling out a poor chump like me.'
His tone held boyish awe and astonishment.
'I see,' said Poirot. He nodded thoughtfully. 'Yes – I see.'
'Why can't Jackie take it like a man?' demanded Simon resentfully.
A very faint smile twitched Poirot's upper lip.
'Well, you see, Monsieur Doyle, to begin with she is *not* a man.'

Check
How do you know that Linnet is rich?
Why didn't Simon stay with Jackie?
What do you think 'Take it like a man' refers to?

Unit 9

🎞 Listening

Listen to this conversation between a policeman and the driver of a car which has been involved in a road accident. The policeman is asking the driver for details of the accident.

1. Make a list of the questions **the policeman asks.**

2. Record the questions and answers in reported speech, like this:

The policeman asked him

> if he …
> what he …

The man said he …

Writing

Write a short report for a local newspaper, reporting the accident. Use reported speech where possible. Start like this:

An accident took place last night in Gordon Road between a … and a …. The driver of the … a Mr … said that he …. When asked if …, he said that ….

Oral exercises

1. Reporting an interview

You are a young gymnast. A reporter has just interviewed you. Report his questions to a friend.

What questions did he ask you?
First he asked me how old I was.

And then?
Then he asked me if I had won any competitions yet.

Here are the reporter's questions:

How old are you?
Have you won any competitions yet?
When did you first become interested in gymnastics?
Did your parents encourage you to take it up?
How many hours a day do you train?
What time do you go to bed?
Do you have to eat any special food?
When do you do your school work?
Which gymnast do you admire most?
Are you hoping to be in the Olympic team?

2. Reporting speech (1)

Choose from these verbs of speaking and report what you hear.

apologise   explain   complain
admit   suggest

'I'm sorry I didn't phone you.'
He apologised for not phoning her.

'You see I couldn't find a telephone that worked.'
'All the phone boxes in the area have been out of order for weeks.'
'Anyway, why don't we go out for the evening?'
'Actually, I don't have a lot of money on me.'

3. Reporting speech (2)

Gerry is going off on a three-month business trip abroad. His girlfriend, Kate, is going with him to the airport.

Listen and then write down the way the words are spoken.
Choose from these expressions:

she said quickly   he said angrily   she said quietly

he said gently   he said impatiently   she said sadly

she said politely   he said nervously

'Oh, do hurry up Kate, my plane leaves in an hour!'
  he said impatiently.

'Do you realise this is our last evening together?'
'Oh, for heaven's sake, Kate, don't start that now!'
'I'm sorry.'
'Listen, I'll write to you as often as I can.'
'That will be nice.'
'Kate... you... you are all right, aren't you? You won't do anything stupid?'
'Yes, yes, I'm fine. Come on, let's call a taxi.'

4. An afternoon out (Open exercise)

Talk to Sandy. Follow the instructions in bold type.

SANDY: Hello! Isn't it a lovely day!
YOU: **Agree** *(Yes, beautiful.)*
SANDY: Can you find somewhere to sit? I'm sorry this room is so untidy.
YOU: **Disagree** *(No, it isn't. It's fine.)*
SANDY: Well, I've got the afternoon off. Where shall we go?
YOU: **Suggest a place to go**
SANDY: Sorry, I didn't quite catch that.
YOU: **Repeat what you said**
SANDY: Where is that exactly?
YOU: **Explain**
SANDY: All right. That sounds fine. But I must go to the bank first and I've got all these letters to post too.
YOU: **Offer to help**
SANDY: Oh, that's kind of you. Thanks. Well, shall we meet in half an hour then?
YOU: **Agree and say goodbye**

Learning checklist

In these units you have learnt how to:

Unit 6

1. Make polite requests using
   'Do you think you could …' and
   'Would you mind …?'

   Do you think you could come and look at it?
   Would you mind signing your name, please?

2. Make arrangements and definite predictions
   using the present continuous and 'will' future

   I'm working in Studio 14 at 11 o'clock.
   I'll be free at 12.

3. Make offers and promises using 'will' and the
   1st conditional

   I'll fix it for you.
   If I'm away, I'll get someone else to do it.

Unit 7

1. Give advice using the 2nd conditional

   If I were you, I'd stay at the Penta Hotel.

2. Discuss consequences of actions using the 1st
   and 2nd conditionals

   If you take the motorway, you'll get there before
     dark.
   If you lived in Bristol it would be cheaper.

3. Put yourself in imaginary situations using the
   2nd conditional

   If I found £5 on the street, I'd hand it in to the
     police.

Unit 8

1. Report requests using 'ask' and 'tell' and the
   infinitive

   She asked me to come and see her.
   She told me to meet her for lunch in an Italian
     restaurant near work.

2. Report statements using 'say'

   She said she was disappointed in me.
   She said I wouldn't get a promotion.

Unit 9

1. Report questions using 'ask' + 'if' or 'wh'
   question words

   She asked me if I liked sport.
   She asked me which sports I liked best.

2. Report speech and behaviour using verbs of
   speaking and adverbs of manner

   He apologised for being late.
   He interrupted her, saying that …
   'No, no!' he exclaimed.
   'Don't go yet,' she said gently.

Rocky Rendezvous

Special 8-day tour of the Rocky Mountains (dep. Vancouver: June 16th, 30th; July 14th, 28th; Aug 11th, 28th)

Offer

Day 1 Vancouver/Victoria
We leave Vancouver and take the ferry across to Vancouver Island. A coach takes us across the island past Campbell River to Kelsey Bay where we pick up an overnight steamer to Prince Rupert.

Day 2 Prince Rupert/Terrace
On arrival in Prince Rupert, we reboard our coach and drive on to Terrace, British Columbia. ⊢⊣

Day 3 Terrace/Prince George
Heading for Prince George, we follow the picturesque Skeena River through miles of mountains and green vegetation. ⊢⊣

Day 4 Prince George/Jasper
Today we see some of Canada's most beautiful scenery, including Mt. Robson, the highest of the Canadian Rockies. ⊢⊣ two nights.

Day 5 Jasper
Trip to Jasper Sky Tram and afternoon free to relax and explore the sights. ⊢⊣

Day 6 Jasper/Banff
This morning we leave Jasper and head south to Banff. On route we stop at the Columbia Icefield where we take a 3-mile long ice-field trip in a snowmobile. ⊢⊣

Day 7 Banff/Vernon
We continue southwest to Vernon, nestled in the Okanagan Valley. ⊢⊣

Day 8 Vernon/Vancouver
Heading further west we return to Vancouver in the early evening.

⊢⊣ = overnight stay in a hotel except on Day 1 where accommodation will be on the steamer.

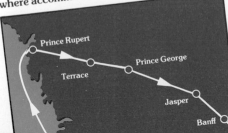

Mr. S. Bates,
75, Tufnell Road,
Wandsworth,
London, SW16.

Jetsave
The Transatlantic Holiday People
Jetsave Ltd
Bridgewater House
South Croydon
Surrey CR2 6AG

Dear Mr. Bates,

I enclose your tickets London–Vancouver return, departing from Gatwick on Sunday June 10th.

Trains to Gatwick leave Victoria every fifteen minutes. Please make sure you check in forty-five minutes before departure time.

At your request I also enclose information about the 8-day tour of the Rocky Mountains. You can make a definite booking in advance or on your arrival in Vancouver.

I wish you a very pleasant holiday.

Yours faithfully,

L.D. Peters

L.D. Peters

Check

When are the Bates leaving for Vancouver?
What special trip are they going on while they are in Canada?
How are they crossing over to Vancouver Island?
Where are they spending the night on Day 1?
How are they travelling most of the time?
What are they seeing on Day 4?
How long are they staying in Jasper?
What are they doing on Day 5?
How are they travelling along the icefield?
When are they returning to Vancouver?

Complete this letter that Mrs Bates sent to a friend of hers, Tricia, before they went to Canada. Write the correct form of the verbs in brackets.

```
                    75, Tufnell Road,
                    Wandsworth,
                    London, SW16.
                    June 5th 1980
Dear Tricia,
      I'm so sorry I haven't written
to you earlier to thank you for
your invitation on July 1st. I'm
afraid that date is impossible for
us. As I think I told you, Stanley
and I (go) to Canada for four weeks.
We (leave) on June 10th and we (not
be) back until the middle of July.

      I remember that you once said you
had relations in Vancouver. If you
(like), I (certainly try) to contact
them for you. Let me know their
address and telephone number. If I
(not have) the time to see them, I
(write) them a note and give them
your love.

      We (stay) with my niece, Sally
while we (be) in Vancouver, but we
(also go) on an 8-day tour of the
Canadian Rockies. It sounds a
wonderful trip. We (stay) overnight
at different hotels on the way and
we (visit) Vancouver Island, the
Rockies of course and we (even go)
on an icefield trip by snowmobile.
We (be) exhausted by the end of 8
days, I'm sure, but we can take it
easy the rest of the time.

      As you can imagine, we're both very
excited about it. Anyway, I(send)
you a postcard from the Rockies when
we get there. See you at the end
of July.

      Love from us both,

      Marge
```

Writing

1. Write the postcard which Mrs Bates sends to Tricia from Jasper.

2. Write a letter to a friend outlining your plans *either* for a holiday or special outing, *or* telling him/her about an important future event in your life, like moving house, changing your job etc.

Game: Guess how I said it!

In groups. One of you chooses an expression from the following list:

quietly
angrily
politely
sadly
in a friendly way
rudely
quickly
in a frightened voice

The others in the group must ask you to make requests in the way you have chosen, like this:

Ask me to turn on the light.
You: Could you turn on the light please? (*politely*)

Try to make your request sound polite (or rude or friendly and so on).

Here are some requests the others can choose from:

Ask me…
to clear up the room
to keep quiet
not to spend more than £10
to help you with your homework
not to tell the police
to post a letter for you
not to be late

The others must try to guess as quickly as possible the expression which describes the way you are speaking.

DISC JOCKEY TELLS OF TEARFUL MESSAGE
Phone Call from Nikos

A teenager claiming to be Nikos, the 17-year-old hunted gunboy, phoned a commercial radio station last night and said, 'I want to be caught.'

Disc jockey Mike Allen of London's Capital Radio said the boy told him he was speaking from a house in Shropshire.

And, said Allen, the boy went on, 'The whole business went wrong. I don't want to be on the run. I want to be back at school.'

Nikos Dimitriou has been on the run for six days, since an incident during which shots were fired at police. He is thought to be armed with a pistol and a shotgun.

Capital Radio is convinced the call was not a hoax.

Allen, 34, said, 'He was sobbing, and at times incoherent. He said he wanted to be caught but he was not going to give himself up, because that would be losing face. It would make him look a cissy in front of his friends.'

In the end the boy sounded close to tears as he told Allen, 'I've got to talk to somebody. I've nobody to talk to.' He rang off, saying, 'They'll be tracing the call. I'm going now.'

Allen went on, 'I asked him if he was sleeping rough or managing to eat, but he just said, "I'm doing OK."

He told me he was desperately sorry about the shooting incident. I asked what he would do if he had the chance to relive the last few days, and he said he would be back at school.'

The call, taken in an 'off the air' studio, could not be recorded.

When the boy hung up, Allen contacted the police.

Check

Who is Nikos?
Why is he wanted by the police?
Why did he ring the disc jockey?
How would you describe Nikos' state of mind when he rang?
Why doesn't he want to give himself up?

Reconstruct as far as possible the conversation between Nikos and the disc jockey on the phone. Use your imagination where necessary. Start like this:

NIKOS: Hello.
ALLEN: Hello. This is Capital Radio, Mike Allen here. Who's calling?
NIKOS: Nikos. Nikos, you know.
ALLEN: Nikos Dimitriou?
NIKOS: Yes. I… I wanted to speak to someone.
ALLEN: Where are you speaking from, Nikos?

The Nicky doll project

Redex Ltd manufactures a large range of toys, including dolls. In the last few years they have had serious competition from other doll manufacturers. Now, in the eighties, they are planning to manufacture a boy doll called Nicky which they hope will sweep the market. The marketing manager, Roger Mason, calls a meeting in spring to discuss the progress of the project. He has invited a market research consultant to the meeting to advise them on the potential market for the Nicky doll.

Background facts	
Existing dolls	*Retail price*
Wanda, Amanda, Lucy, Candy	from £6– £15
*Belinda – laughs and cries	£16.50
*Laura – laughs, cries, talks and sings	£24.50
Under research	*Suggested price*
*Nicky (boy doll) – walks, talks, cries, laughs, sings and kicks a football	£35.00
* = batteries needed	

Present at the meeting:

Roger Mason – Marketing Manager and Chairman
Ron Blake – Sales Manager
Sue Baldwin – Head of Research and Development
Keith Lowry – Production Manager
Angela McCall – Market Research Consultant

Agenda

1. Introductions
2. Market potential and price
3. Competition with existing range of dolls
4. Production schedule
5. Any other business

Divide yourselves into groups of 5. Take one of the roles described above. Read your role description on the next page and prepare what you want to say at various points in the meeting.

Useful language:

Mr Chairman, could I make a point here …
I agree with … I don't agree (disagree) with …
If we …, we'll/we won't …
If we …, it would/wouldn't …

Roger Mason – Marketing Manager

The Nicky doll was your idea in the first place. You have a feeling that boy dolls are soon going to be very fashionable. You are also impressed by the technical side of the doll and what it can do. However, you still feel that you may be taking a risk. If people don't buy the doll, you will lose a lot of money. You are very interested to hear what the market research consultant has to say. You are determined to get the doll into the shops for Christmas.

Ron Blake – Sales Manager

You are not very keen on this doll. You are already selling more than a million low-priced dolls a year, and the battery-operated Laura doll is selling very well at £24.50. You are worried that the Nicky doll will be too similar. If the Nicky doll is successful, it will reduce the sales of the Laura doll. You have spoken to the warehouse manager who says that he has 400,000 Laura dolls in the warehouse at the moment. If he doesn't sell them at Christmas, he will have storage problems and the company will lose a lot of money.

Sue Baldwin – Head of Research and Development

You are very proud of the Nicky doll. You have spent a lot of time working out a way of co-ordinating all the different functions. The kicking mechanism is, however, causing a problem and you have a lot more work to do on it. Because you have many other projects to work on, you don't think you will complete the work on Nicky until the beginning of November. This will mean losing the Christmas market. You think the kicking mechanism is an attractive feature and you think it would be a pity to manufacture the doll without it. You do not agree with the sales manager that Nicky and Laura are similar.

Keith Lowry – Production Manager

Your main concern is to produce efficiently. You are worried about the Nicky doll because it is very complicated and difficult to put together. If they decided to abandon the kicking mechanism, there would be fewer assembly problems and you would be able to reduce prodution cost by £3. Another problem is that you do not think you will have a free production line in October. The only solution would be to run down an existing line. You suggest the Laura doll line.

Angela McCall – Market Research Consultant

From past experience you know that the people who buy most dolls come from the lower income groups. They are prepared to pay up to £25 for a doll but not more. The size of this potential market is very large. However, your research shows that there is not a great interest in boy dolls among this group. Among the higher income groups, who can afford £35, there is definitely more interest. The size of this market is, however, much smaller. You estimate it at about 500,000. You think that Redex might attract some of the lower income groups if they lowered the price.

Activities

1. Note down the main decisions which were taken at the meeting.

2. Construct an advertisement for the Nicky doll to put in a magazine *and* a short TV commercial advertising its special features.

Read the following discussion which took place at the end of the summer in the office of Roger Mason, the Marketing Manager.

MASON: I'd just like to know the present position regarding the Nicky doll. How's the research going, Miss Baldwin?

BALDWIN: I've completed all the necessary tests and there don't seem to be any problems now.

MASON: Good. And the kicking mechanism?

BALDWIN: Er… I'm afraid we decided in the end to abandon it.

MASON: Oh. Pity.

BALDWIN: Yes. But I just didn't have the time, and Keith seemed to think it would be less complicated without it.

LOWRY: Yes, and it is going to bring down production costs too.

MASON: I see. So we can bring down the price, can we?

LOWRY: Yes, I'm doing some calculations and I think we may be able to lower the price to just under £30.

MASON: And how do you think that will affect the sales of the Laura doll, Mr Blake?

BLAKE: I don't know. It may do but it's too early to tell yet. We had a large order from Germany for the Laura doll so I'm a bit happier about the situation.

MASON: Good. Well, is there a free production line now, Mr Lowry?

LOWRY: Yes, I had a talk to Ron about running down the Laura line but he suggested the Belinda doll instead. If you remember, we've been having problems with that one.

MASON: Yes, I do remember. Well, that seems quite satisfactory. Can we get the Nicky doll into the shops for Christmas then?

LOWRY: Yes, I think so. We can start production in… let's see… in two weeks' time.

MASON: Fine. That should give us plenty of time. Well, thank you very much everyone. If there are any further problems, let me know.

Write a report of the meeting under these headings:

Research
Design modifications
Price
Effect on sales of existing dolls
Production line
Production schedule

Start like this:

Research

Miss Baldwin said that she had completed.....

Dave

Dave, the youngest of the Bates children, is in the sixth form at Mayfield Comprehensive in Wandsworth. He is 16 and about to sit his 'O' level exams in the summer. Although he is fairly bright, his teachers think he is lazy and far too interested in out-of-school activities.

Dave's girlfriend, Carol, is a year older than him. She left school last year and is now working as a hairdresser's assistant. They meet once or twice during the week and on Saturday evenings when they go to pop concerts or discos. 'But discos aren't really my scene,' says Dave.

Speedcycling is, however, and Carol often has to take second place. Dave is a member of the Wandsworth Wanderers' Cycling Club. He has a second-hand bike which his father calls a 'death trap'. He spends most of his pocket money on new accessories for the bike and most of his spare time tinkering with it and going on practice runs with his friends from the club.

He still lives at home with his parents. He is very critical of his family. Of his parents he says, 'dad just bosses mum around. I don't know why she puts up with it.' Of Richard he says, 'He's got such a boring job. Just travelling around selling things to put in offices.' And of Sandy, 'She's stupid. She thinks she's going to make it in television. Huh. Some hope!'

Dave's main ambition is to leave school, earn some money of his own and buy a new speed bike.

Check

Make notes on the following:

Dave's school career
His girlfriend, Carol
His interests and hobbies
His opinion of his family
His ambition

Now, without looking at the text, tell your partner what you know about Dave, using your notes.

Unit 11   Dave is angry

It is 7 o'clock on a Saturday evening. Dave is waiting for his girlfriend, Carol, to arrive.

DAVE: Where's Carol? She said she'd be here by 6.15.
MRS BATES: Well, she isn't here. She might have missed the bus.
DAVE: We're going out though!
MRS BATES: She may still be at home. Why don't you give her a ring?
DAVE: No, I rang her half an hour ago and there was no answer.
MRS BATES: Then she must have missed the bus or something. Or she could be in the bath.
DAVE: Well, she's a damned nuisance.
MRS BATES: You know, she might have stopped off on the way to see her sister in Putney. I wouldn't worry if I were you.

Check

Why is Dave worried about Carol?
Is she still at home?
What other possible solutions does Mrs Bates suggest? (that she might/could have ...)

📼 Listen and answer

Why does Dave get angry with his father?
Do you think Dave really cares if Carol turns up or not?

Discuss

Do you think Dave's father was teasing him in a friendly or an unfriendly way?
Do you think that Dave's relationship with his father is quite normal for someone of his age?
Why do *you* think Carol hasn't arrived yet? Make some suggestions of your own.

Dictionary work

Look up the following words in your dictionary:

bored   teasing   reassuring   kind   angry
sarcastic   insensitive   sympathetic
off-hand   rude

Which adjectives best describe the mother's attitude and which best describe the father's?

Set 1

Degrees of certainty: present and future

Uncertain	More certain	Certain
Perhaps she's at home.	She's probably at home.	I'm sure she's at home.
She may/might/could be at home.	She must be at home.	

Australia – the hard way

Barry and Trish Browne, both aged 26, who live in Queen's Road, Richmond are going to reach Perth, Western Australia in February next year 'come hell or high water'.

This is not an ordinary trip for Barry and Trish, because they are doing things the hard way – driving 16,000 km (10,000 miles) overland in 'Nancy', their 1938 Austin 8 motor car. They hope to average 160 kilometres (100 miles) a day. That might not sound very much, but remember that

Barry Browne, however, will have to do most of the driving because Trish is not allowed to drive in Moslem countries such as Eastern Turkey, Iraq, Iran and Pakistan.

Just before they set off on Monday, Barry was as optimistic as usual: 'We've tried to think ahead and to anticipate any and every problem which may arise. Apart from that we are using the motto of the Boy Scouts— Be Prepared.'

even if they pass through Iraq, Iran and Afghanistan safely, the difficult task of crossing the Himalayas will still be ahead of them.

But they are certain of overcoming any problems which may arise, even the 3,600 metres (12,000 ft.) climb to Srinagar in Nepal. After all 'Nancy' has a top speed of 120 km/h (75 mph) and is still going strong after 41 years on the road.

1. **In pairs, discuss the sort of problems that Barry and Trish may meet on their overland journey to Australia.**

2. **Suggest to someone who does not know your area very well where he or she might be able to buy the following:**

a foreign newspaper
second-hand books
tourist souvenirs
China tea
jeans
local cheese
leather gloves
flowers

Start like this:
You may/might find some … at …
or:
They'll probably have some …
at ….

Make a list of your suggestions.

Set 2 Degrees of certainty: past

Uncertain	More certain	Certain
Perhaps she's lost the way. She might/could have lost the way.	She's probably lost the way. She must have lost the way.	I'm sure she's lost the way.

1. Richard went shopping yesterday and lost his wallet. Suggest where and how he might have lost it.

Here are his movements in detail:

– he went shopping at the local supermarket
– he paid for the goods and put his wallet on top of the shopping trolley
– he doesn't remember what he did with the wallet after that
– he packed the goods into a cardboard box
– he carried the box to the car and put it on the back seat
– he drove to the dry-cleaner's, got out of the car and left the car unlocked
– he went to the dry-cleaner's but they told him that his cleaning wasn't ready
– he walked across the road to the greengrocer's to buy some vegetables
– when he came to pay for the vegetables, he couldn't find his wallet.

Work in pairs and make your suggestions, like this:

He Somebody The cashier A person in the shop	might could must	have	put dropped left found	it …

2. Can you solve the mystery?

Read this newspaper cutting about two mysterious tracks in the Alps. Work in pairs and try to give your own solutions to the mystery.

Note: *furrows* are deep tracks in the ground
gouge means to cut roughly and deeply

The mysterious appearance of two huge parallel furrows in the earth of a small valley, high up in the Alps above Nice, is puzzling French scientists. For nobody can explain how they came to be in a place which is completely inaccessible to car or tractor. What are they? What caused them?
The photographs, taken by police officers, show the scene. The furrows start near a crag and gouge their way across the valley in a huge curving arc 63 metres (70 yards) long. Each furrow is 17½ centimetres (7 inches) wide and 25 centimetres (10 inches) deep, and they are exactly 1.8 metres (6 feet) apart along their entire length. Small boulders, rocks and pebbles in the path of the furrows have been almost pulverised.

Contrast

Contrast in speaking	Dave's fairly clever, *but* his teachers think he's lazy.
Contrast in writing	He is fairly clever *but* his teachers think he is lazy.
	Although he is fairly clever, his teachers think he is lazy.
	He is fairly clever. His teachers think he is lazy, *however*.

1. Roleplay. Work in pairs. Use Dave's report to discuss his progress at school. One of you is Dave's class teacher, the other is Mr or Mrs Bates. Start your discussion like this:

MR/MRS BATES: And how is Dave getting on in English?

TEACHER: Well, he has some imaginative ideas. He finds it difficult to write them down, though.

MR/MRS BATES: Oh, I see. And how about French?

Ask also about his progress in History, Mathematics and Science.

2. Write the Headmaster's general report on Dave. Use although **and** however **to link the ideas, like this:**

Although Dave has improved his weaker subjects, he stills needs discipline.
or
Dave has improved his weaker subjects. However, he still needs discipline.
or
He still needs discipline, however.

WANDSWORTH COMPREHENSIVE SCHOOL

Class report 6C   **Name** David Lindsay Bates

English	Has imaginative ideas but finds it difficult to write them down.	
French	Speaks fairly fluently - needs to concentrate more on his written language.	
History	Shows interest in class. Could do very well - must do more homework	
Mathematics	Understands the principles but has difficulties in applying them.	
Science	Has shown a lot of progress this term but still finds it difficult to concentrate	
General Report	David has improved his weaker subjects but he still needs discipline. He also needs to spend more time on his homework and revision. He has the ability to do well but he needs to show more determination. Socially, David is a good mixer and gets on well with everyone. He is a very popular member of the sixth form but he should try to put his studies before his out-of-school activities.	SM.

Development

The Great Pyramid

Cheops' pyramid was 147 metres (474 feet) high on a base 230 metres (759 feet) square. It contained 2½ million blocks of stone, each weighing about 2½ tonnes.

To the people of ancient Egypt, life on earth was short. Life after death, however, was eternal. Therefore they built their tombs of stone and they took their possessions with them into another world.

The more important the person, the greater the tomb. The Pharaohs' tombs were the largest and the most impressive of all: the Pharaohs were the rulers of the country and when they died they became gods. Many of their tombs remain, and some have become a wonder of the world.

These are the pyramids.

The purpose of these huge stone mountains was to protect the burial chamber from the weather and from thieves who might try to steal the gold, jewels and precious possessions placed there to accompany the dead ruler into eternal life.

Their shape, with four triangular sides spreading from a single point, represented the rays of the sun connecting Ra, the god of the sun, with the dead ruler.

Their position on the west bank of the River Nile was where the sun set every day and where they believed it began its journey into the other world. All the burial grounds in ancient Egypt were on the west bank of the river.

At Giza, across the river from Cairo, the ancient Egyptians built the greatest tomb of all: the Great Pyramid of King Cheops.

Check

Why did the people of ancient Egypt build tombs of stone?
Why did the Pharaohs have special tombs?
What were these tombs called?
What was the purpose of them?
What did their shape represent?
Where were they situated and why?
Which is the largest?

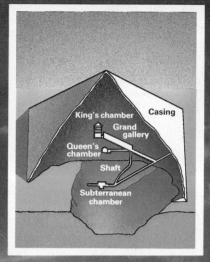

In 820, Abdullah Al Mamun, an Arab prince, tried to discover the secret of the Great Pyramid. He assembled a large number of engineers and stone masons and searched for the entrance. He couldn't find it.

So, with great difficulty, Mamun's men cut a passage into the solid rocks of the pyramid. They discovered a large chamber and a stone sarcophagus. The chamber and the sarcophagus were completely empty.

Had robbers entered the tomb hundreds of years before? If so, how? Or had they built the huge pyramid around an empty chamber? Perhaps the pyramid was not a royal burial chamber. It might have had some other purpose.

The mystery remains. Why did the ancient Egyptians build this fantastic monument?

In groups, discuss possible answers to these questions:

1. Who built the Great Pyramid? How?
How long do you think it took them?
Where did they find the stones?
How did they transport them?
How did they build the pyramid so high and so accurately?
2. What do you think was the purpose of the Great Pyramid?
How could anyone have robbed the chamber and removed the valuable possessions?

Use language like this:

They might/could have …
They must have …
It must have …
I'm sure they …

🔊 Listening

Listen to the tape. You will hear a sequence of sounds and voices. Note down what you think is happening as you listen.

In groups, discuss your version of the story. Use phrases like:

| It | might | |
| That | may | be … |

| He | could | |
| She | must | have been … |

Writing

Write an account of the story. Start like this:

'It was a dark, stormy night. Gerry and Liz were …'

Now listen to the second part of the tape.
Find out what really happened.
Compare your version with the real one.

🔊 Listening

Listen to Paul telling a strange story. Can you think of a logical explanation for it?

Discuss

Have you had or do you know anyone who has had similar unusual experiences? If so, tell your group.

Oral exercises

1. Drawing conclusions

I rang Gerry but there was no answer.
Oh, he must be out then.

I saw a light on in Janet's bedroom.
Oh, she must be in then.

I heard music coming from Mark's room.
There was no answer when I rang Mary's doorbell.
Malcolm's car wasn't outside his house.
There were lights on all over the Newtons' house.

2. Discussing possibilities (About Mrs Bates)

Look at Marjorie Bates' diary for this week.

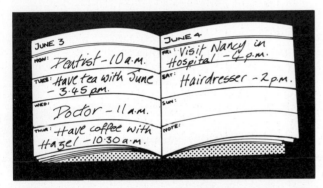

Oh, Dave? Where's your mother? I said I'd ring her today, Monday, at 11.
I'm not sure but she might still be at the dentist's.

Do you know where your mother is Dave? I said I'd call today, Tuesday, at 5 p.m.
I'm not sure but she might still be having tea with June.

Where's your mum Dave? I said I'd meet her at 12.15.
Have you any idea where your mother is Dave? We arranged to meet at 11.30.
Where's Mrs Bates? We were expecting her at 6 p.m.
Dave, this is Auntie Jean. Where's mum? She said she'd be here by 3.30.

3. Discussing possibilities (About Carol)

Where's Carol? Wasn't she going to meet you? Perhaps she forgot.
Yes, she may have forgotten but it's unlikely.

Perhaps she missed the bus.
Yes, she may have missed the bus but it's unlikely.

Perhaps she's had an accident.
Or perhaps she went to see her sister.
Maybe she felt too tired.
Or perhaps she just decided not to come.

4. Discussing possibilities (About Stanley)

Stanley has lost his wallet. Marjorie is suggesting where he might have lost it.

Didn't you put it on the counter when you changed your cheque?
You're right. I might have left it in the bank.

But wait! I'm sure you had it when you bought the meat.
You're right. I might have left it in the butcher's.

But wait! I'm sure I saw it when we took the clothes to be cleaned.
But wait! I saw you take it out when you paid the bill at lunch.
But wait! You paid for the vegetables with a £5 note.
And I remember you paid the paper bill.

5. Rejecting possibilities (About Sandy)

Sandy has not arrived at a friend's birthday supper. It is 7.30 in the evening.

Perhaps she hasn't finished work yet.
But she must have finished work!

Perhaps you didn't tell her the right day.
But I must have told her the right day!

Maybe she didn't have the right address.
Or she may have wanted to ring you and she didn't have your phone number.
Possibly she didn't realise it was your birthday.
Well, she probably didn't get your letter.

Unit 12 Dave takes a risk

Check

What three points should cyclists check?
When can cyclists use public roads for practice racing?
What should they wear on their heads?
What should they write in the club book?

▶ Listen and answer

Dave goes out for a practice run with a friend, Ron, one Saturday afternoon. They go on a busy public road called the South Circular. Dave nearly has a serious accident. Listen to Dave and Ron talking to Mike Palmer, the club trainer, after the accident.
What happened to Dave?
Is he all right?
What happened to his bike?
How did Dave and Ron get back to the club?
How did Mike Palmer react?
What club rules did Dave break?
   (He didn't wear a …)
Does Mike Palmer show any sympathy with Dave?

Discuss

Do you agree with Mike Palmer?
Why do you think young people enjoy speedcycling?
Do you think cyclists are a danger to other road users?

Set 1 Criticism of past actions

Criticism of things not done

He	should / ought to	have worn a crash cap.

| He | shouldn't / oughtn't to | have cycled on the South Circular |

---

1. Look at the Wandsworth Wanderers' Cycling Club rules on the opposite page and in pairs work out what Dave should have or shouldn't have done. (What Dave ought to have or oughtn't to have done.)

Firebug Freddie

2. In pairs, discuss what Freddie should or should not have done in each situation.
(Note: you can use ought to have **and** oughtn't to have **as well)**

3. Private Confession!
Think back to your activities over the past week and make a list of some of the things you think you should have done **and** should not have done.

Choose one of each and 'confess' to your partner.

Friendly criticism of actions

| You needn't You shouldn't | have | bothered to bring brought | flowers. You *are* kind. |

1. Gill has gone to spend a few days with her married friends, Roger and Jane Brinton. Gill is very polite, considerate and generous. She also hates causing an inconvenience.

Write down the missing parts to the conversation below and then read it in pairs.

GILL: Hello! I'm here.

JANE: Gill! come in. How lovely to see you!

GILL: Here. These are for you. You'd better put them in water.

JANE: . . . . We've got plenty in the garden.

GILL: I know. But they looked so nice in the shop.

JANE: Well, thanks anyway. Here, let me take your bag. Phew! It's heavy. What's in it?

GILL: Oh, only a few books and toys for the children.

JANE: But Gill, they've got masses of toys. You really . . . . presents for the children you know. Still, you'll be very popular with them.

GILL: And these are for my bed. They'll save you some laundry.

JANE: . . . . brought your own . . . .

GILL: Well, I have! And here's something to have with our dinner. Let's put it in the fridge to get nice and cold.

JANE: . . . . us a present. Still, it will go very nicely with the fish. Come on, let's go and find Roger and the children.

2. Act the situations

A friend comes to stay with you. What would you say in the following situations? One of you is the guest, the other is the host or hostess.

1.

2.

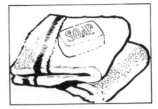

3.

4.

5.

6.

Cause and result

You're *so* keen to go cycling He's *such* a careful cyclist	that	you never check your bike! he's never had an accident.

One fine Sunday, Gill, Richard's girlfriend, decided to take Kevin and her sister's two children down to the south coast to spend a day at the seaside. However, the day was not a success. This is what Gill wrote in her diary that night.

SUNDAY 16 JUNE
What a day! Lovely and hot
decided to take kids to coast.
Late leaving - roads very busy. Car
hot... Kids felt sick all the way.
Very beautiful day - everyone had
some idea. Lots of hold-ups on
road - didn't arrive till lunchtime.
Beach crowded - nowhere to sit.
Sea cold - kids didn't want to
swim. Typical! Kids bored
with beach - went to the Fun
Fair! Long drive home -
decided to leave at five.
children hungry. Again!
Stopped for hamburgers and
ice-creams. Really good to
get home.

1. Make statements about cause and result, like this:
It was so hot that she decided to take the children to the coast.
or
It was such a hot day that she …

Write out the diary entry in full sentences.
Link them where possible with some of the sentence-openers below.
Anyway …   I suppose …   Of course …
When we go to …   Just to make things worse …
In the end …

Start like this:

It was such a hot day on Sunday that we decided to take the children to the coast. Of course, we were so late leaving that …

2. Think up your own results for the following situations:

1. I was so hungry that …

2. I was so bored on the journey that …

3. It was so hot on the beach that …

4. It was such a large building that …

5. The meal was so expensive that …

6. The room was such a mess that …

Development

The Fastnet Disaster

One of the most important events in the yachting season is the Fastnet race. The course is 968 kilometres (605 miles) long, from the Isle of Wight, off the south coast of England, to Fastnet Rock, off the south coast of Ireland, and back again.

On Saturday 11th August, 1979, over 300 yachts started off from the Isle of Wight. On Monday, 13th August, freak gales hit the Fastnet area causing the worst disaster in the history of yacht racing. Fifteen people died and more than twenty-five yachts were abandoned or lost.

THEY SHOULDN'T HAVE RISKED IT

As the death toll in the Fastnet sea disaster rose to fifteen last night, one dazed survivor admitted sadly, 'We should never have risked it.' Californian sailor, Tom McLoughlin, said, 'They warned us three days ago that there would be Force Eight gales. Many of us hoped that the weather would improve. Some continued after it was clear that it was pointless to do so.'

Peter Cross, district officer at the South Wales Coast Guard station said, 'Many of the yachtsmen have only themselves to blame for the disaster. Some of them were not even wearing life jackets.' But, as one critic said afterwards, 'I can't understand why the Racing Club didn't call off the race when they heard the first reports of the disaster.'

Gale forecasts went unheard

A spokesman for the Meteorological Office said that on Saturday, the day the race started, they had forecast Force Eight gales for the area on Monday. And about six hours before disaster struck, a 'gale imminent' warning was broadcast.

Unfortunately, they issued the gale warning at 6.05 p.m. just after the regular shipping forecast had gone out.

Most yachtsmen cannot listen to the radio constantly so they only tune in to regular forecasts. This meant that few heard the warning of a gale until they were actually into really heavy weather. In fact, the gale hit near-hurricane force.

Too little experience

Many of the small yachts were sailed by less experienced yachtsmen, people who were totally unprepared for gales and who had rarely, if ever, handled a yacht in stormy off-shore racing conditions.

When speed can outstrip safety

The tragic disaster of the Fastnet race is likely to be the subject of an inquiry by Britain's Royal Ocean Racing Club. The questions they will ask are:

– Are modern yacht designers concentrating too much on speed by building yachts lighter and lighter so that they are unstable in heavy storms?
– Why do they only test these yachts electronically on shore? Why do they not test the mast and rudder for strength in stormy conditions at sea?
– Why do yachts only have to carry radio receivers and not transmitters?

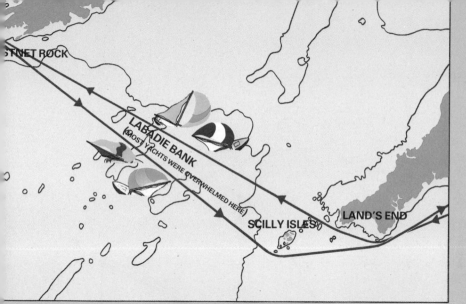

STNET ROCK

LABADIE BANK
(MOST YACHTS WERE OVERWHELMED HERE)

SCILLY ISLES

LAND'S END

Discuss

Discuss in groups whom you think
was to blame for the disaster, and
why. Make notes under the
headings:
The yachtsmen
The Meteorological Office
The yacht designers
The Ocean Racing Club

Use language like this:

They should/shouldn't have …
It should/shouldn't …

Protecting your home

When people leave their houses, either for short or long periods, they often leave tell-tale signs for burglars which show that they are not at home.

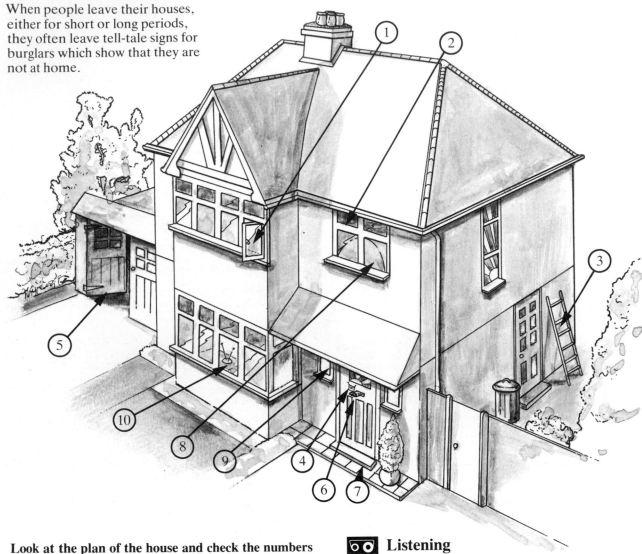

Look at the plan of the house and check the numbers against the list of 'tell-tale' signs below.

Check on the numbers...

1. Windows left open.
2. Windows left unlocked – might as well leave them open!
3. Step-ladder left outside.
4. Note left on door saying 'Back in five minutes'.
5. Garage door left open.
6. Newspapers not cancelled.
7. Keys left under doormat.
8. Money left in drawer, on dressing-table or under mattress.
9. Light left on in hallway. This fools nobody. It's better to leave the sittingroom light on.
10. Valuable items like hi-fi and TV left in full view from front room window.

Listening

Mr and Mrs Bates are going away for the day. Listen to them getting ready to leave.

1. Decide which of the 10 tell-tale signs they left and make a note of them.

2. Note down or report to the rest of the class what they should or shouldn't have done in each case.

Writing

Imagine you are the secretary of an amateur sailing club *or* an amateur mountaineering club. Make a list of safety precautions for the club members. Think of the following areas: clothing, equipment, weather, experience.

Oral exercises

1. Admitting mistakes

A burglary has happened at your house.

I can't understand why you didn't lock the back door.
Yes, I know I should have locked the back door.

And it seems you left the kitchen window open.
Yes, I know I shouldn't have left the kitchen window open.

And you were mad to leave a note on the door.
And you didn't cancel the newspapers.
Why did you leave all that money on the table?
And you didn't close the garage doors, either!

2. Making excuses (Open exercise)

Did you pay the gas bill?
No, I know I ought to have, but I couldn't find (my cheque book).

Did you phone June?
No, I know I ought to have, but I couldn't find (her phone number).

Did you write to the Wilsons?
Did you repair the kitchen table?
Did you telephone the TV repair shop?
Did you do the shopping?

3. Expressing misunderstandings (1)

Look at Exercise 2 again. This time answer like this:

Did you pay the gas bill?
No, should I have? I thought you'd paid it.

Did you phone June?
No, should I have? I thought you'd phoned her.

4. Expressing misunderstandings (2)

I paid the rent today.
Oh, shouldn't you have paid it last week?

And I wrote to the bank manager about the cheque.
Oh, shouldn't you have written to him last week?

What else? Oh yes, I returned the library books.
And I took the car in for service.
Oh yes, I went to the dentist's too.
And I telephoned about the central heating.

5. Reporting results

Report what you hear.

'I'm so tired I don't think I'm going in to work.'
She was so tired that she didn't go in to work.

'I'm bored with the party. I'm leaving.'
He was so bored with the party that he left.

'I'm still hungry. I think I'll have another piece of apple pie.'
'I was so excited I didn't sleep all night.'
'I didn't realise I was so thirsty. I've drunk a whole litre of milk.'
'I'm sorry I shouted. It's because I'm upset, that's all.'

6. Stating results (Open exercise)

Have you seen the new Bertolucci film?
No, but it sounds such an interesting film that I thought I might (go and see it tonight).

You haven't got the new 'Blondie' album, have you?
No, but it sounds such an interesting album that I thought I might (buy it).

You haven't been to the arts and crafts exhibition, have you?
Have you been to the new Greek restaurant in the High Street yet?
Have you read the latest Alastair MacLean novel?
You haven't seen the new *Hamlet* production at the National Theatre yet, have you?

Unit 13 Dave has a problem

Dave and Carol are in a hamburger restaurant in Putney, near Wandsworth.

DAVE: I still don't understand why you had to see your grandmother on Saturday evening.

CAROL: Well, it was a family thing. I'd completely forgotten about the concert. Anyway, my mum would have been upset if I hadn't gone.

DAVE: She wouldn't have been surely. She'd have understood. You could have told her you had tickets for a concert.

CAROL: I said I forgot! And you haven't phoned me at all during the week. If you'd phoned me on Friday night, I wouldn't have forgotten.

DAVE: But you know I go training every Friday night.

CAROL: I'm sorry… but it's just that I wish you wouldn't take me so much for granted.

DAVE: But we always go out on Saturday evenings.

CAROL: That's just it! Oh, sometimes I wish I'd never started going out with you. You act as if you own me.

Check

Why didn't Carol turn up at Dave's last Saturday evening?

Why did she feel she had to go to her grandmother's?

Does Dave agree with her?

Did Dave phone her on Friday evening? Why?

What does she feel about their relationship now?

📼 Listen and answer

Why does the waitress irritate them?

Why is Dave particularly angry that Carol forgot about the concert?

Discuss

Do you think Dave sees Carol's point of view?

Is she being reasonable?

What do you think will happen to their relationship?

Criticism of people and places

I wish you wouldn't take me for granted so much. (habit)
I wish I didn't have red hair. (fact)
I wish we had a canteen at school.

What Annoys You Most?

So . . . you think you're the only one who has parents that expect you to wash up . . . the only one whose boyfriend forgets to turn up on dates . . . WELL . . . we know that we all share the same problems. Find out for yourself.

Fill in below what **annoys you most** about your friends, family, yourself and your home town. Then buy next week's magazine and see just how common your criticisms and complaints really are.

The boy in my life	My parents	Myself	My home town
Lives in another town. Doesn't have a car. Takes me for granted. Doesn't take me out to discos, but only to the cinema.	Complain about my room. Criticise my clothes. Don't give me enough pocket money. Always blame me for everything. Haven't got a nice garden.	I'm shy when I meet new people. My hair's a boring colour. My feet are too big.	There's no disco. There's not enough to do. It's not close enough to London. Everyone knows what everyone else is doing.

1. A young girl has filled in her own opinions. Imagine that she is saying, not writing, what she thinks. Express her criticisms, like this:

I wish he | lived in the same town.
 | didn't live in another town.

I wish | my parents wouldn't always criticise my clothes.
 | I wasn't so shy when I meet new people.
 | there was a disco in our town.

2. In pairs, ask each other what annoys you about people you know at work, school or at home, like this:

How do you get on with your …?
Oh, he/she is/they're all right, but I wish …

and your home town, like this:

How do you like living in …?
Oh, it's OK but I wish …

Past hypothesis

If you *had rung* me on Friday night, I *wouldn't have forgotten.*

Thanking their lucky stars

Here are those lucky people who, from sheer coincidence, were not on the hi-jacked Jumbo Jet to New York...

'My wife fell seriously ill on the day I was meant to go.'

'My car broke down on the way to Heathrow Airport so I missed the flight.'

'I wanted to go on that flight but it was full up.'

'Our New York office rang and postponed our meeting for another week.'

'My secretary booked me on to the wrong flight, luckily.'

'I had a night-mare that something terrible was going to happen and I took a later flight.'

1. Imagine you are these people. Explain your lucky coincidence, like this:

'I would have been on that flight if my wife hadn't fallen ill on the day I was meant to go.'

2. The following newspaper cuttings describe incidents that could have been avoided. In each case, explain how, by using
'If... had/hadn't..., ... would/wouldn't have ...

Mother angry at son's death
The mother of a youth who hanged himself in hospital told the Coroner's Court on Tuesday. 'The nurses didn't watch him properly. He could still have been alive today with proper care and attention.'

'The new hospital is a scandal,' said Councillor Hatton. 'They should have spent the money on basic hygiene equipment like sterilisation units, but they wasted it on expensive and unnecessary electronic equipment.'

'We believe that the financial assistance from the government was a bad policy decision. Without this aid, *British Motors* would have learnt how to stand on their own two feet.'

Said disappointed tennis star McEnroe last night, 'Losing an important point in the fourth set cost me the match.'

Mrs Patricia Hayes, mother of the two-year-old boy, said, 'We didn't put safety catches on the windows because I never realised he could climb up that far.'

Mr Thomas, speaking on behalf of *Sun Tours* denied that they had misled tourists. 'Nowhere in the brochure does it say that the Hotel Casablanca is situated on or even near a beach. If people don't bother to read the brochures properly, they can only blame themselves.'

Does a good education really matter?

We went along to Wandsworth Job Centre and surveyed some people to find out how important they felt that a good school education was.
The results showed that many people were disappointed in their education. They put the blame sometimes on the school and sometimes on themselves. Many felt that their teachers were not good enough, that many of the text books were out-of-date, especially when it came to science, and that they should have had more or better careers advice. They also felt that they should have been made to work harder, either by the teachers or by their parents. But people seemed equally ready to put the blame on their own shoulders. Many felt that they had chosen the wrong subjects when they started to specialise, or that they had wasted time at school. Others felt that they had left school too early in their eagerness to get a job and earn money. A few even thought that their failure was due to the type of school they went to, and that they would have been better off somewhere else.

3. Imagine that you are one of the people chosen for the survey. What did you actually say?

Make your criticisms like this:
I wish I had had a better Maths teacher
or
I wish I hadn't wasted so much time at school.

Work through all the criticisms and regrets in the same way.

4. Now link possible causes to these consequences. Complete the sentences in any way you like:

I would have got into university if
…
I might have passed my exams if
…
I could have gone to medical school if …
I would have got a much better paid job if …

5. Work in pairs.
Ask your partner if he/she has any criticisms or regrets about his past life, anything that he would or might have done differently in different circumstances.

Development

Surely it couldn't happen here...?

It had been a difficult decade, the eighties. The constant economic crises had taken their toll. In 1987 the government had closed down the public bus service and many railway lines, so that cars and heavy lorries were coming into central London at the rate of 200,000 a day.

Earlier, in 1984, the government had stopped the construction of the Thames Flood Barrier and there was no money to maintain and check the flood warning alarms along the banks of the Thames.

The government had also postponed the building of a new power station to provide extra power in emergencies. Power for the underground trains, and for the whole traffic light system, still came from the old power station on the banks of the Thames at Lots Road in Battersea.

It had been a lovely summer, that summer of 1989. The long, sun-soaked days seemed to go on forever. The autumn was good too, with the best grain harvest for 25 years.

Then winter came. It was the worst winter for 50 years. The blizzards started in the middle of January and the snow fell continuously for over a month. Cattle and sheep died. Great drifts of snow covered the country and cut off towns and villages.

At the beginning of March the snow began to melt. It rained non-stop for six days and people began to gather on the banks of the Thames as the level of the river grew higher and higher.

The Thames flows right through the centre of London. Its waters rise and fall with the tide. The spring tides in the North Sea are always heavy, but that year they were exceptional. They were made even worse by storms and gales.

On the night of March 7th a northerly gale began to send a huge surge of tidal water right into the mouth of the Thames just as the river was running high.

No, surely not? It couldn't happen here. Could it?

The people of London were used to misfortune. They accepted the bad weather, and even the three-month-old railway strike. Good times, they said, must be just round the corner.

The early morning rush hour started. Thousands of commuters packed themselves into the underground trains. Parliament Square station, close to the Thames, was particularly busy that morning with civil servants hurrying to their offices in Westminster despite the weather.

At 8.50 a.m. the Thames burst its banks – at Lots Road, at Westminster Bridge and at Waterloo Bridge.

By 9.00 a.m. nearly 2 metres (six feet) of water covered 9½ square kilometres (six square miles) of central London. The streets were impassable. There was no electric power. There was no light. The gas mains were exploding. People could not get out of their homes, their cars or the underground trains. Twenty thousand people either drowned or were injured by falling buildings.

By 9.15 a.m. London was drowning.

1. Work in pairs. Analyse the disaster. Make notes about the causes which led up to it under the following headings:

Natural (e.g. the weather)
Economic and political (e.g. economic crises)
Technical (e.g. power station)

2. Make notes on what happened when the Thames burst it banks.

3. Explain how the catastrophe could have been avoided. Link the facts from 1 and 2, like this:

If they hadn't closed down the bus service and …, there wouldn't have been so many cars …

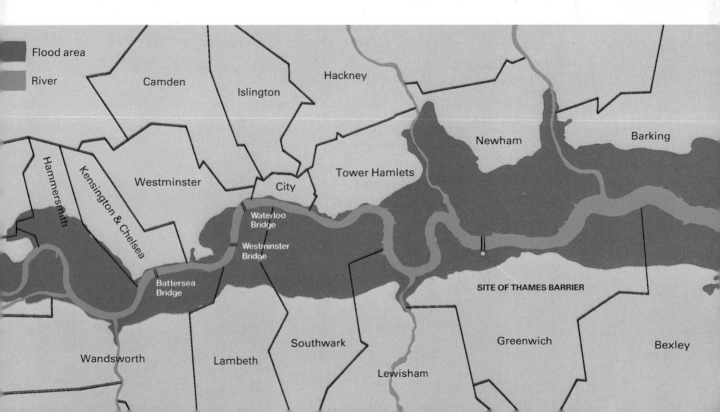

Flood area
River

Camden
Islington
Hackney

Hammersmith
Kensington & Chelsea
Westminster
City
Tower Hamlets
Newham
Barking

Waterloo Bridge
Westminster Bridge
Battersea Bridge

SITE OF THAMES BARRIER

Wandsworth
Lambeth
Southwark
Lewisham
Greenwich
Bexley

🔊 Listening

Listen to Evelyn talking about an incident which occurred in the Negev desert during her holiday in Israel.

As you listen, note down exactly what happened. Comment on the events and the decisions which Evelyn and her friend made like this:

If they had/hadn't, they would/wouldn't have …

Writing

Complete this letter that Evelyn wrote to her family from her hotel in Jerusalem.

The American Colony
JERUSALEM
July 10th

Dear June,
    Jerusalem is an amazing city. Our hotel is very old, very attractive and beautifully cool. I'm writing this after getting back from a hair-raising trip in a hired car. We had quite a narrow escape, in fact what happened was this ……

Oral exercises

1. Expressing envy

We've got a house in the country, actually.
Really? I wish I lived in the country.

But I'm going abroad to work next month.
Really? I wish I was going abroad to work.

Yes, I'm going to Mexico.
And also I've got friends in Jamaica.
They have a house by the sea.
I'm lucky. My job involves a lot of travelling.

2. Criticising people

Mr Bates is talking to his wife about Dave's plans.

By the way, Dave says he's going to be out for lunch.
Well, I wish he'd tell me when he's going to be out.

And he is having his friends in for the evening.
Well, I wish he'd tell me when he's having his friends in.

And by the way, he's asked Carol home for a meal tomorrow evening, too.
And he says he's going to be away for the weekend.
And I also forgot, he says he's going to be at the club all day tomorrow.
And he's bringing the whole cycle team home for supper tonight.

3. Criticising your parents

Look at page 103. You are the girl who filled in the questionnaire.

How do you get on with your parents?
Oh, all right. But I wish they didn't always complain about my room.

What else do you find irritating?
Well, I wish they didn't always complain about my clothes.

Anything else?

4. Expressing regrets

Anna, a friend of Sandy's regrets some decisions she has made.

Do you regret leaving school so early?
Yes, if I hadn't left school so early things would have been different.

And do you regret not getting any qualifications?
Yes, if I'd got some qualifications, things would have been different.

Do you regret getting married so soon?
And do you regret having children immediately?
And it's a pity you didn't go back to your job.
And I can't understand why you moved house.

5. Giving excuses

Rephrase the excuses.

I'm sorry I didn't phone but I was in such a hurry.
Sorry, I would have phoned if I hadn't been in such a hurry.

I'm sorry I was late but I lost the way.
Sorry, I wouldn't have been late if I hadn't lost the way.

I'm sorry I didn't come but I had such a bad headache.
I'm sorry I was rude but I was tired.
I'm sorry I missed your party but I was delayed at work.
I'm sorry I didn't let you know earlier but I lost your telephone number.

6. Commenting on circumstances

Comment on the fatal circumstances leading to the London Flood Disaster:

If only the winter hadn't been so bad!
If only the spring tides hadn't been so high!

1. Bad winter.
2. High spring tides.
3. Government stopped building the flood banks.
4. Rail strike.
5. Power station near the Thames.
6. Not enough money for the flood alarm system.

Unit 14   Dave protests

World wild life facts

The seal...

Every year, 50,000 baby seals are slaughtered in the annual seal cull. Sometimes they are shot, but mostly they are clubbed to death. Last year, in Canada alone, more than 40,000 were killed and their pelts made into sealskin coats, hats and handbags.

Dave has recently joined a protest group concerned with the conservation of wild life. He takes part in a demonstration outside a large London department store during the annual sales when fur coats are sold cheaply.

WOMAN: Live animals! Not fur coats!
MAN: Stop! Think! Don't destroy the world's wild life!
DAVE: Madam, do you know why we're protesting outside this store?
WOMAN: It's something to do with fur coats, isn't it?
DAVE: Do you know how many animals are killed to make one fur coat? Do you know what happens to baby seals, for instance?
WOMAN: They're put to death painlessly, aren't they?
DAVE: They're clubbed to death. Out on the ice. They are taken from their mothers, chased across the ice, and then beaten to death with clubs.
MAN: Come off it mate! If they aren't controlled, they'll eat all the fish. They have to be killed.
DAVE: They don't, you know. Nature has its own way of control.

Check

Why is Dave protesting outside a department store in London?
Which animals in particular are they concerned about?
How are these animals killed?
What are the animal pelts used for?

Listen and answer

What is the name of the protest group to which Dave belongs?
What three things are they hoping to persuade people outside the department store to do?

Discuss

Do you think demonstrations of this kind can be effective?
What do you think is meant by 'Nature has its own way of control'?
What other forms of sea life are being threatened? How?

Processes

| The biscuits *are packed* into containers |

This is how biscuits are made

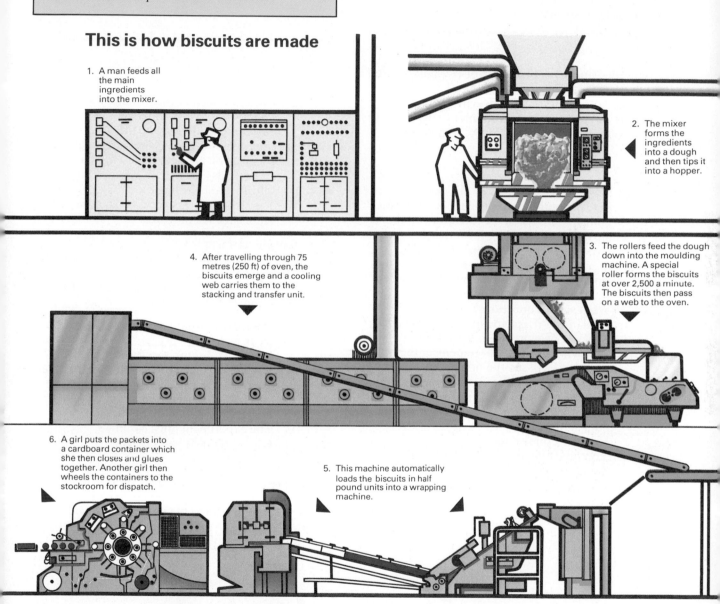

1. A man feeds all the main ingredients into the mixer.

2. The mixer forms the ingredients into a dough and then tips it into a hopper.

3. The rollers feed the dough down into the moulding machine. A special roller forms the biscuits at over 2,500 a minute. The biscuits then pass on a web to the oven.

4. After travelling through 75 metres (250 ft) of oven, the biscuits emerge and a cooling web carries them to the stacking and transfer unit.

5. This machine automatically loads the biscuits in half pound units into a wrapping machine.

6. A girl puts the packets into a cardboard container which she then closes and glues together. Another girl then wheels the containers to the stockroom for dispatch.

1. Read the description of how biscuits are made and follow the diagrams as you read. Write a paragraph explaining the process using the passive form of the verb. Start like this:

All the main ingredients are fed into a mixer. They are formed into a dough by the mixer and …

2. In groups, work out one or two of the following processes:
– how a letter reaches your doorstep
– how a record is produced and distributed
– how tea is grown
– how a house is built
– how something becomes a law in your country.
Use dictionaries and reference books if necessary.

111

Objective reports

Several people from the street *were asked* to take part in an experiment.

In 1963 an American professor of psychology from the University of Yale decided to test how far people responded to authority. He advertised for people to take part in a 'learning experiment'. Here is an account of the way one man, Mr X, responded.

MR X: So how much of a shock do I give him?
PROF. M: Well, look at this meter.

15 v	150 v	300 v	450 v
slight shock	bad shock	severe shock	danger X

PROF. M: Now Mr X, the point of this experiment is to test whether people learn better if you punish them when they make a mistake. I have chosen two people for this experiment – yourself and Mr Y here. Now I am going to put Mr Y in a booth – he already knows what he has to do. Now, would you please stand here and ask him questions.
MR X: What sort of questions?
PROF. M: Well, first I'd like you to read a list of about 30 pairs of words like BLUE-BIRD or PRICE-LIST. Mr Y must try to remember them. Then you will say the first part of the pair and Mr Y must tell you the other half. So when you say BLUE he must say BIRD. If he says BEARD or BELL he is wrong and you punish him.
MR X: How do I punish him?
PROF. M: You give him an electric shock each time. You can see that I have wired up Mr Y with pads on the side of his head. Right? Now this machine here can give electric shocks ranging from 15 to 450 volts.

Each time he makes a mistake you give him a shock of 15 volts and it goes up 15 volts each time all the way up the scale.
MR X: I see. And what does the shock feel like?
PROF. M: I'll give you an idea. This is what a 15 volt shock feels like.
MR X: Oh! Just a slight tingle.
PROF. M: Yes. Nothing very serious. Shall we start? Here's the list of words.

The experiment started. Mr Y made mistakes and Mr X gave him stronger shocks each time. Mr X could see from Mr Y's face that the shocks were starting to cause him pain. Mr X reached 250 volts when suddenly Mr Y jumped up.

MR Y: Stop! I can't stand any more. I've got a weak heart.
MR X: Professor, I think we should stop.
PROF. M: I'd like you to continue with the experiment please.
MR X: But I don't want to. This man has got a bad heart. The shocks might kill him.
PROF. M: The experiment must continue.
MR X: Oh, all right. If you say so...

In fact, Mr Y was not a genuine subject. He was an actor. He never received any shocks during the experiment. He only acted as if he was. He increased his expression of pain as the voltage increased.

The results of the experiment can be shown in the following diagram:

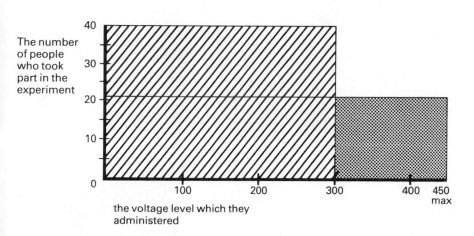

The number of people who took part in the experiment

the voltage level which they administered

Answer these questions.

1. Who was the experiment conduted by? (It was conducted by an American.)
2. What was the experiment really designed to test?
3. Who was chosen as a subject for the experiment?
4. What was Mr X told that the experiment was for?
5. Where was Mr Y placed for the experiment?
6. What was Mr X told to do first?
7. What was he asked to do when Mr Y made a mistake?
8. How were the electric shocks administered?
9. By how much was the electric shock increased at each mistake?
10. What did Mr Y say he was frightened of?
11. What happened when Mr X wanted to stop giving the shocks?
12. What, in fact, was Mr Y asked to do at the beginning of the experiment?
13. How many subjects altogether were chosen to do this experiment?
14. How high a voltage were they all prepared to administer?
15. How high a voltage werc 20 of them prepared to administer?

Now write an account of the whole experiment, using the questions and answers above as a guide. Start like this:

An experiment, designed to test ... ..., was conducted by an American professor from ... People from the street were ... ... Here is an account of what happened during one typical experiment. Mr X and Mr Y were asked into the laboratory. Mr X was told that ...

Discuss

In this experiment ordinary people were prepared to inflict pain on other ordinary people just because they were ordered to by a person in a position of authority.

What do you think are the political, social and educational implications of the results of this experiment?

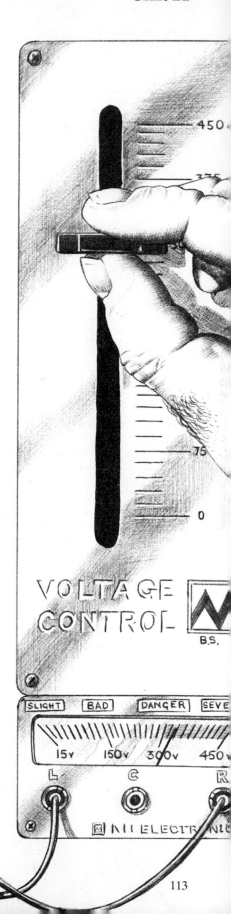

Development

The Game of Life

Sabrina Wentworth-Brown 'born with a silver spoon in her mouth'. One of three children in an Admiral's family. Educated at a private school and at a finishing school in Switzerland.

Sharon Chambers, an only child. Father a doctor, mother a social worker. Educated at an expensive public school in Sussex.

Kelly Kovacs, the son of Polish immigrants to Britain. Educated at local grammar school. Parents hard working in their own delicatessen shop.

Blake Gillespie, one of seven children. Brought up on a big housing estate in south London. Father a railway porter, mother an office cleaner. Educated at the local comprehensive.

The rules of play

Two can play

1. Choose one of the four characters and read the facts about his or her background.
2. Throw the dice for each part of your 'life'. Each number represents a different situation.
3. When the dice falls each time, write down your OWN result. Discuss the circumstances and the possible reasons for each situation your throw of the dice reveals. Build up the story of your life.

4. Before 'The Final Throw' (section 5) use your notes to talk about yourself and justify some of the things that have happened to you.
5. Make the final throw of the dice. Note down what happens to you and work out an explanation in your defence.
6. In groups of 4 or 5, either present the case for your defence or give an apology with reasons. The others must decide what is to be your fate in the game of life.

The way the dice fall...

1st throw
...at school

1. You are made to repeat a year for failing your exams.
2. You are expelled for cheating.
3. You are made Head Boy/Girl of your school.
4. You are injured in a moped accident just before your exams.
5. You are given distinctions in your final exams.
6. You are elected President of the school debating society.

2nd throw
...at the start of your career

1. You are advised to take a job in a catering firm.
2. You are turned down for several interviews and are now washing up in a hotel.
3. You are offered a job by a record company.
4. You get a job in an advertising agency but you discover that you hate it.
5. You are accepted as a management trainee in a large business firm.
6. You get a good job in the travel industry but you are disliked by the people you work with.

3rd throw
...during your first year

1. You are made redundant and are forced to take a low-paid job in a restaurant.
2. You are given encouragement and more responsibility at work.
3. You are arrested at an open-air pop concert for noisy behaviour.
4. You are fined for drunken driving and you lose your licence.
5. You become an active union member, and elected branch secretary.
6. You are given a substantial increase in salary.

4th throw
...in your personal life

1. You have a steady relationship and are soon to get engaged.
2. You have to spend most of your free time looking after your sick mother.
3. You are given a marvellous birthday party by your colleagues at work.
4. You are thrown out of home after a family row.
5. You are left a large sum of money by a rich relative to buy a house.
6. You are very upset by your parents' decision to get divorced.

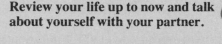

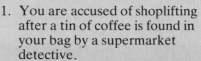

Review your life up to now and talk about yourself with your partner.

Final throw
...in the end

1. You are accused of shoplifting after a tin of coffee is found in your bag by a supermarket detective.
2. You are arrested for obstruction and for causing a public nuisance during a demonstration against racialism.
3. You are arrested at Heathrow Airport with a false-bottomed suitcase containing 200 Swiss watches.
4. You are charged with careless driving after a road accident.
5. Your home is raided by the police; after a search they discover some stolen jewellery hidden behind a bookcase.
6. You are charged with theft at your work place after a colleague's wallet is found in your coat.

What will be your fate? Will you win or lose in the Game of Life?

Writing

Either write up the case for your defence *or* a probation officer's report on your case.

Unit 14

🎧 Listening

Divide into two groups.

Group A:
Listen to the following news report from the radio. The report contains four different items. While you listen make a note of the most important facts about each item.

Group B:
Look at the following 'skeleton' of the news. Construct questions which will give you the relevant information to fill in the gaps. When Group A has finished listening, pair up with one member of that group and ask him/her the questions. Write out the full report filling in the missing information as you go along. Compare your version with that on tape afterwards.

1. Thousands of police and secret service men were alerted yesterday after a threat to .... and ... were found in an apartment in New Jersey. A letter delivered to ... stated .... It was said to come from ....

2. A man was called in for questioning by the police yesterday in connection with ... in which two policemen .... He was released after eight hours' questioning on the grounds of ... .

3. Plans to ... are to be drawn up by the Greater London Council although they have been warned that .... A former leader of the GLC said that one of the most costly problems to be solved is .... would need to be vastly improved before such a scheme could be accepted, he said.

4. ... have been announced by the European Commission in reply to criticism that .... In future, guests of the Common Market will have to be satisfied with .... A suggestion that there should also be ... has been rejected.

Writing

Either
Study the most important news items from a national newspaper in your country and write a short radio news report.
or
Write a short news report about the most important events in your school/place of work or local area.

Oral exercises

1. Apologising for faults

Can I use this cup?
I'm afraid it's cracked.

Can I wear your jacket this evening?
I'm afraid it's torn.

Choose from these verbs:

tear   scratch   stain

break   crack   burn

Can I use your hairdryer?
Can I have some toast?
Can I put this record on?
Shall I use this table cloth?

2. Understanding a process

Listen to this man explaining how biscuits are made.

This man feeds the ingredients into the mixer.
I see. The ingredients are fed into a mixer. Then what?

Then the mixer forms them into a dough.
I see. They're formed into a dough. Then what?

Then the mixer tips it into a hopper.
Then a roller makes it into biscuits.
Then the biscuits pass into an oven.
Then a cooling web carries them to the stacking unit.

3. Confirming reports

A friend of yours is looking at a newspaper you have already read.

Did you know, they've caught the bank robbers!
Yes, I knew they were caught.

And they found the stolen money.
Yes, I knew it was found.

By the way, they *did* shoot the policeman.
Oh, and they've settled the Steel Strike.
What else . . . oh yes, they've cancelled the Miss World Competition.
And look, they've released the hostages.

4. Reporting an accident

You receive this letter from a friend.

Dear John,
I don't suppose you've heard about Max's accident? Well, he was driving along the M1 when a lorry hit him from behind. I don't know how it happened. Anyway, he was thrown out of his car. An ambulance arrived almost immediately and took him to hospital. Apparently he injured his legs. The doctors operated on him immediately and then transferred him to the local hospital. They only discharged him last week.
Awful isn't it! . . . .

What happened to Max?
He was hit by a lorry on the M1.

And?
He was thrown out of the car.

How awful! Did he go to hospital?
Was he seriously hurt?
So he had an operation?
What happened then?
When did he come home?

5. Reporting news

What's in the news then?
Well, the police have been given a 20% salary rise.

Have they? What else has happened?
Well, a British athlete has been arrested for using drugs.

Has he? What else?

Use these headlines:

1 **Police Given 20% Salary Rise**

2 **BRITISH ATHLETE ARRESTED FOR USING DRUGS**

3 **Missing Schoolboy Found in Hong Kong**

4 **SCHOOL TEACHER ACCUSED OF TAKING BRIBES FROM PARENTS**

5 **New Cure Discovered for Arthritis**

6 **Nurses offered new pay deal**

7 **Buckingham Palace converted into flats**

117

Learning checklist

In these units you have learnt how to:

Unit 11

1. Express degrees of certainty (present and future) using 'may' 'might' 'must' and 'probably'

   He may be reading the paper.
   She might be in the bath.
   She must be on the way.
   She's probably at home.

2. Express degrees of certainty (past) using 'may have' 'might have' 'must have' and 'probably'

   She may have missed the bus.
   He might have dropped it.
   He must have left it in the car.
   He probably left it at home.

3. Express contrast using 'but' 'although' 'however'

   He's good at Maths, but he isn't good at Science.
   Although he's good at Maths, he's not so good at Science.
   He's good at Maths, however, he isn't …

Unit 12

1. Express past obligation using 'should(n't) have' and 'ought(n't) to have'

   He shouldn't have left the iron on.
   He ought to have checked the brakes.

2. Express friendly criticism using 'shouldn't have' and 'needn't have'

   You shouldn't have bothered to bring your sweets.
   You needn't have brought your sheets.

3. Express result of actions using 'so … that' and 'such a … that'

   I was so tired (that) I fell asleep.
   It was such a hot day (that) we went to the seaside.

Unit 13

1. Express criticism and regret using 'I wish…'

   I wish he didn't take me for granted.
   I wish she wouldn't smoke so much.
   I wish I was taller.
   I wish I hadn't left school so early.

2. Discuss past hypotheses using the 3rd conditional

   If my wife hadn't been ill, I would have been on that plane.

Unit 14

1. State facts using the present passive

   A large number of seals are clubbed to death every year.

2. Make objective reports using the past passive

   Two people were asked to take part in the experiment.

3. Describe processes using the present passive and the present perfect passive

   After the biscuits have been cooled, they are packed into containers.

Unit 15 Consolidation

1. NEWS AT ONE
A *news flash*

2. FACE TO FACE
An *interview* with
a well-known
personality

3. A CRITIC'S VIEW
A *discussion* about
a new film or TV
programme

4. THE WORLD ABOUT US
Behind the scenes
at an airport:
interview with
airport official

5. WE ADVISE
A *discussion* based
on 'problem' letters

**This is your chance to make up
your own radio or TV programme.
A programme of news, views and
entertainment.**

Divide yourselves into six groups.
Each group will work on a different part of the programme.

Choose which part of the
programme you would like to
work on and form a group.

Use the information which refers
to your section to help you
prepare your script.

Each part should take about 2 or
3 minutes on the air.

When you have finished
preparing your part of the
programme, select the member
or members of the group who will
present and take part in it.

One of the members of Group 6
will also be the overall programme
announcer and co-ordinator. The
other groups should consult this
person for the order in which the
different parts will be presented,
and give him/her an idea of how
best to introduce your particular
part.

Now turn to the following pages
and find your section.

News At One

Use the following headlines to construct four news items. The questions which accompany the headlines will help you fill in the details for each item. Write out a full script and select one member of the group to read it out.

20 DIE IN HOLIDAY COACH DISASTER

Who was in the coach?
Where was it going to?
When did it happen?
Where and how did it happen?
Which members of the coach party were killed?

Tinned Food Poisoning Scare

What sort of tinned food was it?
How was the poisoning discovered?
What were the effects?
What are the company concerned saying about it?
Have they issued any warning to the public?

HEADMASTER ACCUSED OF BRUTALITY

What is the name of the school head and where is the school?
Who made the accusation?
What sort of brutality was it?
What did the head say?
What measures are the local authorities going to take?

Government Offer Housewives A Salary

Which country is involved?
When will the bill take effect?
How will housewives be paid? (Out of their husband's salary?)
What are the reasons for introducing this?

Face To Face

You are going to interview a writer of some best-selling children's books. The writer is called Katie Garrett.

Make up a list of questions to ask Katie Garrett. The questions should concern:

her own childhood and background
her education
her interest in writing
why she writes children's books in particular
her writing career up till now
what her books are about
which age group they appeal to
why she thinks they sell so well
any lucky coincidences that have happened to her
any regrets she may have over her past life.

Arrange the questions in the most appropriate order.

Now make up imaginary answers to these questions, as if you were Katie Garrett.

Write out a full script and select two members of the group to present it. One will be the interviewer, the other will be Katie Garrett.

A Critic's View

Choose a recent film or television programme. Select a member of the group to introduce the film or programme. He/she must give the title, say who the director is (if known) and who took the leading parts. He/she must also give a short summary of the story of the film or of the contents of the programme. This will be followed by a discussion. At least two people must take part. You may like to give these people special names and decide what they do and why they have been chosen to take part in the discussion. (They may be film directors or actors or newspaper critics.)

Guidelines for discussion:

I thought it was one of the ... I've ever seen
far more ... than I imagined it would be (give reasons)

I agree/I don't agree ... I liked the way it/they ...
I didn't like the way it/they ... I didn't think ...
I thought it should have ...
I didn't understand why ...

The discussion will sound more natural if you do not write out full scripts. Jot down the points you want to make in note form instead.

The World About Us

The subtitle of this part of the programme is *A Quick Turnaround*.

You are going to interview a Mr Billows, a British Airways maintenance manager. He is going to explain what has to be done from the moment an aeroplane lands until it is ready for take-off again. Help to prepare Mr Billows' script by studying the information below. Write out his script in full. One of you must introduce him and thank him afterwards.

Cleaning staff duties

– remove rubbish
– clean and empty toilets
– vacuum clean carpets and dust tables
– re-stock plane with towels, soap etc.
– bring on food and duty-free goods

Maintenance staff duties

– refuel
– put right any minor fault which the pilots have noted down
– carry out routine check of instruments
– check oil levels and tyre pressure

We Advise…

Your job is to analyse and discuss listeners' problems of all types. One of you must introduce the panel of advisers:

Alan Maingard is a social worker. Sally Hewitt is a careers officer. Julia Lamont has a problem page on a weekly magazine.

For this programme you have chosen two letters. Select two other members of the group to read them out. Deal with each letter in turn.

The panel must prepare an outline of the points they are going to make. Each person must comment at least once on each letter. Make sure that you all have something different to say each time.

You may write a full script if you wish but the discussion will sound more lively and natural if you just have notes in front of you.

Michael is forty-two and I am twenty-one. We have been going out together for eighteen months and I have never before been worried about our difference in ages. But now Michael wants to get married and suddenly I am worried about making our relationship too permanent. For one thing he wants to have children soon and really I would like to wait at least four years before I have to give up my job and stay at home. Also I can't help worrying about what things will be like in say fifteen years' time. Will he seem like someone from a different generation; will he be too old to have a good relationship with his child; will we find that our friends have nothing in common? I have quite oldfashioned ideas about marriage being permanent, but I couldn't bear to be tied to someone who I just felt sorry for or who irritated me in the same way as my father does. You may think this makes me sound very selfish but I am just trying to be realistic. I love Michael very much and can't imagine breaking up.

I am married with two children in their early teens. I gave up work when I had my first baby and I haven't had any paid employment since then. I want to have an interesting life apart from the children now that they are growing up, and I just don't know where to begin. I don't want to return to clerical work which I found very dull, but I don't seem to be trained for anything else. Please help me!

Sharing our Cultures

Are people from different cultures really very different?

Imagine that you have a visitor from another part of the world. How would you explain your cultural background to this visitor? How would you explain the way your people behave socially, in families, at school and at work? Could you explain what your country looks like? Could you explain how the educational system or the government works?

In pairs, or in groups of similar nationality, prepare answers on the topics presented on these pages. Try to make your explanations as clear and simple as possible.

1. Social behaviour

How do you greet someone you know well?

How do you greet someone you don't know?

Does your age or sex make any difference in the way you greet people?

What sort of hand gestures are common? What do they mean?

Do people mind if you are late for an appointment?

Do you usually bring a gift if you are invited to someone's house?

2. Geography and climate

What variations are there in geographical features and countryside?

Describe the variations in climate.

3. Family and marriage

Do families usually live together with their relatives?

What happens to older relatives if they are unable to look after themselves?

Who takes the important family decisions?

If a girl of 16 wanted to go out with a boy alone, what would the parents say?

Does the family have an influence on whom the son or daughter marries?

Are there any special engagement customs?

If a married couple wanted to divorce, would this be possible? How would the family react?

4. Food and eating habits
What main meals are eaten
during the day? At what time of
the day?
Describe what an average person
might have to eat and drink at
these meals.
What special food might you offer
a visitor from another country?

5. Education
Describe the different types of
school available.
Are there any private schools?
Has the educational system
always been like this within
your memory?
How would you compare your
system with any other that you
know well?

6. Work
What are the main industries?
How are people chosen for jobs?
How are working hours
organised?
How are people paid?
Would an employer be able to
dismiss an employee if he was
not satisfied with his work or
behaviour?

7. Literature, arts and religion
Does your country have any
world-famous authors, poets,
artists or musicians?
Are there any other art forms for
which your country is famous?
What are the common religious
beliefs held by your people?
How are these practised?

8. History
Name an important historical
event in the history of your
country. When did it take
place? What happened? Why
was it important?
If it hadn't taken place, what
would have been the
consequences?

9. Government
What political parties are there in
your country?
How is the present system of
government organised?

Texts of extended dialogues
(Listen and answer)

Unit 1 Richard starts again

Listen to this conversation between Richard and his parents. They are discussing his leaving to find a place of his own.

Richard: And how's your day been, dad?
Mr Bates: Oh, not so bad. Got back about four o'clock. I gave Kevin a little ride in the lorry, you know, to give your mother a bit of a rest.
Richard: Yes, I know it's tiring for her having Kevin around. But it won't be for much longer now, I hope.
Mr Bates: Oh? Found something have you?
Richard: Yes, I think so. A small house in Wimbledon. I'll show you the ad in the paper if you like.
Mrs Bates: Now what's all this? You're not really leaving us, are you? The house will be very empty without you and Kevin, you know.
Richard: Mm. And very peaceful, I'm sure. It's tiring having a young child in the house, I know. Besides, you'll be able to go back to work, mum.
Mrs Bates: Oh, don't you worry about that. But what about your job? It's still a long way from Wimbledon.
Richard: I know. I'm going to try and get a job somewhere near Wimbledon if possible.
Mrs Bates: Well . . . if you're sure . . .
Richard: I'm sure, mum.
Mr Bates: Well you must make your own decisions. You know best. Now Marge, what about some more tea? And where's that lad, Dave? It's half past six isn't it? Suppose he's out on that bike of his . . .

Unit 2 Richard settles down

Richard has now bought the small house in Wimbledon and has moved in with Kevin. His mother, Mrs Bates, telephones to find out how they are settling down.

Richard: Hello 3411.
Mrs Bates: Richard? It's mum here.
Richard: Oh, hello mum. Just a second . . . put your jacket on Kevin if you're going out to play . . . sorry mum. How are you?
Mrs Bates: Oh fine. I just wanted to find out how you were settling down.
Richard: Oh, we're still in a bit of a mess, but it's getting better. And Kevin seems to like it here.
Mrs Bates: Oh, that's good. Is there a garden for him to play in?
Richard: Yes, we've got a small garden which is a bit untidy at the moment, but we'll soon sort that out. It's not big enough for him to play football in, but it's all right. And of course, there's Wimbledon Common quite near.
Mrs Bates: And a school? Have you found a school for Kevin?
Richard: Yes, there's one just round the corner. They say it's one of the best schools in the area.
Mrs Bates: That's good. So you like it there, do you Richard? You don't think you've made a mistake moving to Wimbledon?
Richard: Oh, no. It's got everything we need. Shops, cinemas and restaurants. There's even a theatre you know, which people say is very good. And the house isn't very far from the underground station which is useful if we want to go to London.
Mrs Bates: Yes, I can see that.
Richard: The only trouble is going to be in the summer when the tennis traffic is awful.
Mrs Bates: Yes, but it's only for a fortnight, so it won't be too bad.
Richard: No. I suppose you're right.
Mrs Bates: Anyway, I'm glad you and Kevin are settling down.
Richard: Oh, yes we are.
Mrs Bates: It's nice to know that Kevin likes it there. Come over and see us when you've got time. And don't forget I can look after him whenever you want.
Richard: Thanks mum.
Mrs Bates: Give my love to Kevin.
Richard: Yes I will. Bye mum, and thanks for ringing.

Unit 3 Richard gets a new job

Richard goes for an interview at AM-ADMEL and sees Mr Preston, the Sales Manager.

Mr Preston: (voice through intercom) Could you send Mr Bates in now please, Shirley?
Shirley: Right . . . Mr Bates? Mr Preston would like to see you now, if you're ready.
Richard: Oh. Yes . . . right. Thank you. (knocks at Mr Preston's door)
Mr Preston: Come in.
(Richard enters and shuts door)
Ah, Mr Bates. My name's Preston. How do you do. Do take a seat.
Richard: Thank you.
Mr Preston: You had no trouble getting here, I hope?
Richard: No. As a matter of fact, I live in Wimbledon now, so it was very easy get here.
Mr Preston: Good. Now I have your letter here . . . yes . . . so you've had previous experience in selling, I see.
Richard: Yes. I was a sales representative for BSB actually, the office equipment people.
Mr Preston: Oh yes, I know them. Any special reason for wanting to leave?
Richard: Practical reasons really. They're based in Central London and the travelling is too much.
Mr Preston: Yes, quite. Well, from your point of view, a job in Wimbledon would be ideal, I suppose.
Richard: Yes. But you supply other areas in South London I presume?
Mr Preston: Yes we do. Wandsworth, Clapham, Richmond even. We have our contacts but . . . well . . . we're looking for someone with ambition and initiative. Someone who's good at dealing with people and who's able to make new contacts and leads. And to make them faster than our competitors.
Richard: Yes, yes I realise that.
Mr Preston: So, really, though the hours can be fairly flexible, you have to be prepared to work hard in this job, if you want to make a success of it. Perhaps harder than you imagine.
Richard: Well, I'm quite prepared to do that.
Mr Preston: Mm . . . Oh . . . just a routine question. You can drive, can't you and you have a current driving licence?
Richard: Oh yes.
Mr Preston: Good. Well, the next thing is the product. I don't know how much you know about our range but you have to be able to talk about it fairly confidently and demonstrate the machines and so on. Perhaps you'd like to take a look around. Ask any questions you like . . .

Unit 4 Richard remembers

Richard and Gill, a friend from work, are talking after dinner one evening.

Richard: More coffee, Gill?
Gill: No, thanks. It keeps me awake.
Richard: Why don't you put a record on? They're over there on the shelf.
Gill: OK. Is there anything you'd like in particular?
Richard: No, you choose.
Gill: You've got a lot of Abba records I see.
Richard: Yes, my wife used to be very keen on them at one time.
Gill: Oh, did she?
Richard: Mm. And the Bee Gees. She's got all their albums too.
Gill: What happened to your wife, Richard?
Richard: She died in a car accident.
Gill: Oh, I'm sorry. I didn't realise . . .
Richard: It's all right. I don't mind talking about it now.
Gill: How long ago did it happen?
Richard: Last summer. It happened while she was driving home from work.
Gill: Oh, quite recently then.
Richard: Yes, it wasn't long ago.
Gill: How long were you married?
Richard: Seven years. We got married as soon as she left college. I was only twenty. It seems such a long time ago. So much has happened since then.
Gill: Yes, I'm sure. Were things difficult? I mean . . . how did you manage with Kevin afterwards?
Richard: Well, I sold our house and we moved in with my parents. They were marvellous but – well – their house is very small so we couldn't stay for ever.
Gill: So you bought this house?
Richard: Yes. Just a few months ago.
Gill: Don't you feel lonely sometimes?
Richard: Sure. Sometimes.
Gill: I will have just a little more coffee after all.

Unit 4 (Set 2 Exercise 2)

Richard: How long have you worked for AM-ADMEL Gill?
Gill: Only for a year. It's May now isn't it? Yes, I joined last August in fact.
Richard: August '79.
Gill: Yes.
Richard: What did you do before that?
Gill: I used to work for a travel agency in London.
Richard: It sounds interesting. Was it?
Gill: Not really. It was just secretarial work, rather like this job. And it wasn't too well paid. But I took a secretarial course when I left school and I couldn't think what else to do.
Richard: So you went straight from school into a secretarial course did you?
Gill: Well, not quite. I took 'O' levels and left school when I was 16 – in 1972, I think it was. And then I went to work in a hotel in Austria for a year, to learn some German.
Richard: Austria? Why Austria?
Gill: I don't know really. Well, we used to go there on holiday quite often when we were younger – and – well I like Austria actually. Anyway then I went back and did the secretarial course. That was a year's course.
Richard: And then you got the job at the travel agency I suppose.
Gill: Yeah, that's right. That was in '74.
Richard: So you were there five years!
Gill: Yes, it's awful isn't it? Actually, I'm thinking of giving it all up to become a nurse.
Richard: Really?
Gill: Mm. Well, I worked in a hospital in Twickenham during my last year at school. Just cleaning and helping to make beds and so on. It was part of our Practical Careers training.
Richard: And you liked it?
Gill: Yes, it was interesting.

Unit 6 Sandy makes arrangements

(Sandy lifts receiver in office and dials 0)

Sandy: 501 please . . . Oh Mark? . . . Sandy here. How are you? . . . How was last night by the way? . . . You won? Great! . . . Look, I'm afraid there's something wrong with the office video . . . Oh, I don't know, the picture is wobbly. Do you think you could come and have a look at it? . . . Yes, I suppose so. I'm only typing a letter to someone who didn't like last week's 'Close Up' programme . . . Oh, you know, the one about old people in hospitals. Anyway I'll see you in a few minutes then . . . Fine, bye!
(puts phone down)
(Mark opens her door)
Mark: *(in a fruity voice)* You rang madam?
Sandy: *(laughing)* Oh, hi! You sound like that guy in those Dracula movies! Well, the video's over there.
Mark: Look, I'm afraid I haven't got time to fix it now. I'm doing something in Studio 14 at 11 o'clock. But I'll be free at 12. I'll do it for you then. OK?
Sandy: Fine, I'll be here all morning.
Mark: If I can't come at 12, I'll get someone else to fix it.
(Stella, a senior programme assistant, enters)
Stella: Have you finished that letter? . . . Oh!
Mark: I'm trying to fix a time to come and repair the VCR.
Stella: Oh. Well, Sandra, when you've finished making your arrangements, would you mind finishing those letters please. They are important, you know.
Sandy: Yes, Stella.
(Stella goes out and shuts door)
Sometimes she makes me want to . . .

Unit 7 Sandy wants a change

Sandy arrives at Richard's house one evening to babysit for Kevin.

Richard: Oh, hello Sandy. I thought you'd never come!
Sandy: Hi! Sorry I'm so late. We had a meeting at work. Oh, it's all so awful there now!
Richard: Well, leave then! I'd never stay in a job if I hated it. And it's not as if they pay you that well either!
Sandy: Oh, it's not just that. It's all these stupid cuts. Do you know what? They're going to shut the canteen in the morning and afternoon so we can't get tea or coffee there. We have to get it from the machines! They say they'll save money if they don't have to have staff on duty in the canteen all the time.
Richard: Well . . . that's quite true. They will.
Sandy: Yes, but if they shut it we won't have anywhere to sit down and chat. We'll have to drink our coffee in the corridor!
Richard: Mm. But lots of places have that system now.
Sandy: Well I don't think it's worth it. And now they're being mean about the heating too. They're not going to turn it on till the first of October and they're going to switch if off on the first of April. And they're only going to have it at 66 degrees. I mean, what if it's a long hard winter like last year. If it is no one will come in. We'll have a strike. It's awful trying to work when you're cold!
Richard: But they've got to save money somehow, Sandy. What with the energy crisis, they . . .
Sandy: Look! There are hundreds of better ways of saving money. Do you know, if I wanted to make cuts, I'd stop all those expense account lunches at Mama Roma's. *And* I'd make the management staff come in before 10 o'clock!
Richard: Well, I'd raise the whole thing at a union meeting if I were you.
Sandy: Mm. I think I will. But they never listen to us junior staff. Honestly, if I could find a better job, I'd leave tomorrow.
Richard: Would you really, Sandy?
Sandy: Yes, I would.
(door bell rings)
Richard: Oh, that'll be Gill. Look, don't worry Sandy. It's not that bad. It's happening to every large company now, even us!
Sandy: Hm. Where's Kevin?
Richard: Having a bath. I'll just open the door . . .

Unit 8 Sandy reports

Sandy is having lunch with her flat mate in a wine bar in Marylebone High Street.

Val: So. What's new at the office then?
Sandy: Stella – you know the woman at work – asked me to have lunch with her yesterday.
Val: Oh, that was nice of her.
Sandy: It wasn't! She wanted to discuss work – my good points and my bad points. It was for promotion.
Val: What did she say about you?
Sandy: More wine . . . ?
Val: Thanks. Come on Sandy, tell me what she said.
Sandy: She told me to meet her for lunch in a little Italian restaurant near the studio.
Val: Go on.
Sandy: And after we had ordered she told me she was going to be very frank.
Val: And . . . ?
Sandy: She said she was very disappointed in me.
Val: No.!
Sandy: Yes, she did. Then she said she didn't like my attitude. She said I was 'difficult'.
Val: Have some cheese.
Sandy: Thanks. And – she said she wouldn't be able to give me promotion. She even asked if I had thought about getting another job.
Val: Goodness, Sandy, she *was* frank! But surely she can't give you the sack?
Sandy: No, she can't. Anyway, I told her I thought the work wasn't very interesting. Well you know how boring it is.
Val: What did she say to that?
Sandy: Well I think she understood. She said she might be able to find me something different to do.
Val: Like what?
Sandy: Testing audience reaction – you know, asking people if they like certain programmes.
Val: Oh, well, Sandy, cheer up. At least it will get you out of the office.
Sandy: And it'll make a change from typing.
Val: Here, let's finish the wine.

Unit 8 (Set 2 Exercise 3)

Narrator: Monday morning, nine o'clock at LTV.
Stella: Oh, is that you, Sandra? There are one or two things I would like to discuss with you, about work. Would you mind meeting me for lunch tomorrow? So we can have a talk.
Sandy: Oh! Yes, certainly – where?
Stella: Do you know the little Italian restaurant in Chester Street?
Sandy: Yes, yes, I do.
Stella: Well, meet me there at 12.30, could you? I may be a few minutes late but there'll be a table in my name. Ask the head waiter.
Sandy: Right.
Narrator: Tuesday at the restaurant.
Stella: Now you know me well enough Sandra. I always like to get to the point. And…I'm not going to beat about the bush. I'm going to be very frank with you.
Sandy: Yes…yes…go on.
Stella: Frankly Sandra, I'm not very pleased with you. I don't know – it's something about the way you approach your work, your attitude to it, that worries me.
Sandy: Oh really? How do you mean?
Stella: Well, you don't seem to respond to me very well. In fact I find that you're not easy to work with. Yes, really Sandra, I find you rather difficult.
Sandy: I'm sorry you think that.
Stella: The point is – and I think I should be truthful with you, I can't honestly recommend somebody for promotion who doesn't take an active interest in their work. You can see that, can't you Sandra?
Sandy: Er,…yes I can and I'm sorry. I thought I was doing my best.
Stella: Maybe, but you don't seem to enjoy your work. I mean, are you happy at LTV? Perhaps you need a change? Have you ever thought about working somewhere else? You know, a different sort of job.
Sandy: Well, no. It's not that. I like it here. I like working for LTV. I think television is exciting. It's just that my job, what I do, seems so boring, so repetitive. I don't feel as if I'm getting anywhere.
Stella: I see. Yes, I think I understand how you feel. I'm glad you told me. But you've got to realise, Sandra, that we can't *all* do exciting work *all* the time.
Sandy: Yes, I know that.
Stella: Look, this is what I think we'd better do. Bill Fletcher who deals with audience reaction and research wants someone to help him on door-to-door interviews and so on. We might be able to fit you in somewhere there. What do you think about that?

Unit 9 Sandy investigates

(doorbell rings)
Tony: Yes?
Sandy: Oh, good afternoon. I'm from LTV. We're doing an audience survey on our sports programmes. Would you mind answering a few questions? It won't take very long.
Tony: No, sure. Come on in.
Sandy: Thank you. Right. Your name?
Tony: Tony Collins.
Sandy: Are you over twenty-one?
Tony: No, I'm 19.
Sandy: Right. Are you interested in sport?
Tony: Yes, quite.
Sandy: You're quite interested. How often do you watch 'Sportsview'?
Tony: 'Sportsview'. Oh yes, that's on Saturday afternoon, isn't it?
Sandy: Yes, from 1.30 to 5.
Tony: Oh yes. Yes, I watch it sometimes. Depends what else I'm doing. I don't watch it every week.
Sandy: But you do watch it sometimes.
Tony: Yes.
Sandy: Which sports do you prefer to watch? Soccer, rugby, tennis, golf Have a look at the list here.
Tony: Oh right…boxing…no…horse racing never…er…I suppose like watching soccer best of all, then athletics.
Sandy: Fine. Do you think 'Sportsview' is too long, too short or just righ
Tony: I don't know. I mean, I'm not interested in all the sports so I neve watch all of it. Yes, I'd say it's about right.
Sandy: I see…and would you like to see more sport on television during week?
Tony: No, not really. Weekends is enough I think.
Sandy: Right. Thanks very much. That's very helpful. I hope I didn't tak up too much of your time.
Tony: No, no, that's OK. I'll show you out.

Unit 11

It's seven o'clock at the Bates' house in Wandsworth.
It's Saturday evening.

Dave: What's the time?
Mrs Bates: Seven.
Dave: Where's Carol then? She said she'd be here by 6.15.
Mrs Bates: Well, she isn't here. She might have missed the bus.
Dave: We're going out though!
Mrs Bates: She may still be at home. Why don't you give her a ring?
Dave: No, I rang her half an hour ago and there was no answer.
Mrs Bates: Then she must have missed the bus or something. Or she coul have been in the bath.
Dave: Well, she's a damn nuisance!
Mrs Bates: You know, she might have stopped off on the way to see her sister in Putney. I wouldn't worry if I were you.
Dave: Huh! I'm going to have a shower.
Mrs Bates: What if she rings?
Dave: If she does, tell her to hurry up. Otherwise we'll miss the concert.
Mr Bates: I expect she's forgotten about it.
Dave: What do you mean?
Mr Bates: Well, she may have something better to do.
Dave: Like what exactly?
Mrs Bates: No, Dave, she must be on her way. She'll be here soon. She w have forgotten.
Dave: Well, I don't care. She bought the tickets. She's got them. It's her money.
Mr Bates: Well, perhaps she's taken someone else.
Dave: Look, dad, give it a rest, will you! I don't want to discuss it any m
Mr Bates: I was only saying…
Dave: I'm going to have my shower!
Mr Bates: *(calling)* Are you going to stay at home and watch the football the telly with me then?
(door slams)
(the phone rings)

Unit 12 Dave takes a risk

Dave has just had an accident on the South Circular. It is Saturday afternoon. He is with his friend, Ron.

Dave: Oh, my head's bleeding.
Ron: Why didn't you wear your cap? You were dead lucky, you know, Dave. You could have been killed by that truck.
Dave: Yeah, I know. It must have been my brakes. Oh, look at my bike! It's a write-off. I'll never be able to ride it again.
Ron: We'd better get back to the club. I'll ring my brother and ask him to come and get us in his van...

Later at the club. Dave and Ron meet Mike Palmer, the leader of the Wandsworth Wanderers.

Mike: ...and what do you think you were doing out on the busiest road in London at the busiest time of day?
Dave: We wanted a practice run.
Ron: Yeah, just a short one.
Mike: Practice run! If you wanted a practice run you should have gone to the track at Ham Hill.
Dave: But it's so boring there. There's nothing to look at!
Mike: And what's so exciting about the South Circular? Anyway, you don't ride with the Wandsworth Wanderers just to look at the scenery, my lad.
Ron: Dave's bike is a write-off.
Mike: Yes, and he ought to have been a write-off too, by the sound of it! You kids should be more careful. You go out, you don't think, your bikes are joined together with bits of string...
Dave: But I bought it from a guy in the Hounslow Harriers.
Mike: Makes no difference. I don't suppose you checked the brakes before you went out, did you?
Dave: But they were all right last week!
Mike: Last week! It's today I'm talking about. You never take a blind bit of notice of the club rules. You're so keen to get away that you never think!
Dave: I'm sorry, Mike.
Mike: So am I. You should have had a bit more sense, that's all I'm saying. You're like those people who try and climb mountains in running shorts. *And* you didn't check out your route in the book.
Ron: We thought we didn't have to on short runs.
Mike: Well, you *do* have to. We're professionals in the Wandsworth Wanderers, not just amateurs. Now you'd better clean up before your mum sees you. Come on, lad. It's not the end of the world.

Unit 13 Dave has a problem

At Macarthur's a hamburger restaurant in Putney, near Wandsworth.

Dave: I still don't understand why you had to see your grandmother on Saturday evening.
Carol: Well, it was a sort of family thing. Everyone was there. I'd completely forgotten about the concert. Anyway, my mum would have been upset if I hadn't gone.
Dave: She wouldn't have been, surely? She would have understood. You could have told her you had tickets.
Carol: I said I forgot.
Waitress: Are you ready to order now?
Dave: Yes. Two 74s please – one medium and one rare. Oh – and two salads.
Waitress: And to drink?
Carol: Coffee for me.
Dave: Two coffees, please.
Carol: And you haven't phoned me at all during the week. You're too busy with your cycle club. If you'd phoned me on Friday night, I wouldn't have forgotten.
Dave: But you know I go training every Friday night.
Carol: I'm sorry but it's just that...
Dave: What?
Carol: Well, I wish you wouldn't take me for granted so much.
Dave: I don't! Anyway, *you* wanted to go to the concert. You bought the tickets months ago. Anway, we always go out on Saturdays.
Carol: That's just it.
Dave: That's just what?
Waitress: Did you want dressing with your salad?
Dave: What? Oh, no thanks.
Waitress: OK. No dressing.
Carol: Oh, I don't know. It's just...
Dave: It's just what?
Waitress: Two 74s. Whose is the rare?
Dave: Mine.
Carol: Oh, sometimes I wish I'd never started going out with you. You act as if you own me. If only you were a bit more...
Waitress: Is everything all right?
Dave: Fine, everything's fine.

Unit 14 Dave protests

A demonstration outside a large London department store. It is the time of the annual sales when fur coats are sold cheaply.

Voices: We say 'Stop the Slaughter'! We say, 'Stop the Slaughter'.
Girl: Stop killing the seals!
Woman 1: Live animals! Not fur coats!
Man: Stop! Think! Don't destroy the world's wild life!
Dave: Madam, can I have a word with you?
Woman 2: Well...er...I'm in a hurry I'm going to the sales.
Dave: It won't take a moment.
Woman 2: OK.
Dave: Do you know why we're protesting outside this store?
Woman 2: It's something to do with the fur coats, isn't it? They've got some lovely wild fox furs.
Dave: Do you know how many animals are killed to make one coat? Do you know what happens to baby seals for instance?
Woman 2: Well they're put to death painlessly, aren't they?
Dave: They're clubbed to death. Out on the ice. They're taken from their mothers, chased across the ice, and then beaten to death with clubs.
Man: Come off it mate! If they aren't controlled, they eat all the fish. They have to be killed. They have to be controlled.
Dave: They don't have to be killed, you know. It's only the fur industry that says that. Nature has its own way of control.
Child: Look, at that picture of that poor little seal, mummy. It's all covered in blood.
Woman 3: Come away, Sharon. It's horrible!
Dave: That's how the seals are killed. That's the evidence.
Woman 2: Here, I'll sign your petition.
Girl: Boycott this store! Boycott this store!
Boy: Support 'Friends of the Earth'. Support 'Friends of the Earth'!
Dave: Perhaps you'd like to give a donation to 'Friends of the Earth'? You can help stop the world's wild life from disappearing.
Woman 2: Yes, I think I will. But I'd still like to go to the sales.
Dave: One day there won't be any wild animals left in the world. You'll just have plastic ones in Disneyland.

WHEN YOU BUY YOUR NEXT FUR COAT
THINK WHAT HAPPENS
TO THE ANIMAL'S THROAT!

Grammatical summary (Unit by Unit)

UNIT 1   Relative clauses with *who, whose* and *where*
Clauses of purpose with infinitive
with *so that*

UNIT 2   Relative clauses with *which*
There is/are (revised)
Have got (facilities)
Comparative and superlative forms of adjectives
Too and *not enough*

UNIT 3   Modal verbs: *should, have to, needn't*
Comparatives: much + adjective + *er* + *than*; *much more* + adjective + *than*;
just as + adjective + *as*; *not as* + adjective + *as*;
not as + adjective + *as*
Comparative of irregular adverbs: *hard, fast, good*

UNIT 4   Past simple and past continuous
Time clauses with *while, as soon as, before, after*
Time markers: *during, for, since, ago*
Used to (facts and habits)

UNIT 5   Consolidation

UNIT 6   *Do you think you could* + verb
Would you mind + verb (*-ing* form)
Present continuous (future use)
Will (future definite predictions)
1st conditional *If* + present tense/$_{can}^{will}$ + verb

UNIT 7   1st conditional (revised)
2nd conditional *If* + past tense/*would* + verb

UNIT 8   Reported requests and commands: *He asked/told me (not) to . . .*
Reported statements with *say*

UNIT 9   Reported questions with *wh* question words, and *if* + verb change
Reported speech with different verbs of speaking
Adverbs of manner (in speech behaviour)

UNIT 10 Consolidation

UNIT 11 Modal verbs: *may, might, must* + verb
may have, might have, must have + verb
Clauses of contrast, with sentence connectors *but, although, however*

UNIT 12 Modal verbs: *Should, ought to, needn't* + *have* + past participle
Clauses of result: *so* + adjective + *that*
such a/an + adjective + noun + *that*

UNIT 13 *I wish* + past simple
+ *would* + verb
+ past perfect
3rd conditional *If* + *past perfect/would have* + *verb*

UNIT 14 Present simple passive
Past simple passive
Present perfect passive
Passive-derived adjectives, e.g. *cracked, broken*

UNIT 15 Consolidation